Confessions
from your
Fat Friend

PAIGE FIELDSTED

ISBN Print: 978-0-9985469-4-0

ISBN Digital: 978-0-9985469-5-7

Cover Design: Concierge Literary Designs & Photography, LLC.

Editing: Elevated Editing Services

Proofreading: Lawerence Editing

TABLE OF CONTENTS

For McKenna, Emerson, LaRue, Evelynn and little girls everywhere. May you never doubt that you are loved, worthy and enough, just the way you are.

———————————

INTRODUCTION

AM I THE ONLY ONE?

I've been the girl who doesn't fit in all my life. As a young girl, I towered over my classmates, girls and boys, and weighed more than all of them too. I was the first girl to start wearing a bra and got made fun of for it by boys in my third-grade class. I knew early on that I was different from the rest of the girls in my class. I was never going to be the same size as them, and they were never going to "catch up" to me. I felt out of place from the very beginning, from the time I was in kindergarten and all the way through high school. That feeling didn't go away when I got to college or into adulthood. I continued to be the biggest friend in every group. I continued to be the fat friend.

I could never share clothes or shoes with my friends or even go shopping with them. When it came time to have sports uniforms handed out when I was in high school, I always had to wonder if there was going to be one that fit me. At least once, my fear of needing a new uniform ordered just for me came true.

I very clearly remember the first time I knew I was being excluded based solely on my body size. I was in fifth grade, and I was doing a history fair project with four of my classmates. We were doing a skit about the invention of the telephone, and I played Alexander Graham Bell because I could memorize large amounts of the script. At the end of our play, we were going to do a little dance to Reba McEntire's "Why Haven't I Heard from You." The first time we practiced, though, I was left out. I was told by one of the moms that the other girls were going to do the dance and I should stay behind our presentation board. The other girls were all roughly the same size and much smaller than me. I went home crying to my mom, and like she did so many times in my life, she stepped up to the plate for me and called the other mom. The next day when we practiced again, I was included in the dance. I was 11-years-old.

I could tell you dozens more stories like that one. Stories where I didn't fit in, where I was excluded or made fun of, or when my mom had to fight for me because that's what moms do best. But I'll save some of those for the confessions to come.

I think it goes without saying that these are my stories, told in my words and from my unique perspective. But because memory is notoriously unreliable, the people in these stories (other than me, of course) might even remember the events differently. The people in these stories likely had a very different perspective on the situation and had no idea how their comments/actions were impacting me. I didn't write this book to make any of those people feel guilty. I didn't write this book to make anyone feel bad for me or to secretly shame all my haters from years past. Even though I know some of these stories will inevitably make you feel bad for me, I didn't write this book to elicit pity from you.

Although these specific confessions are mine, I don't think I'm unique. I don't think the stories and thoughts and feelings contained in these pages are unique to me. Simply going off of the number of people who have told me, "I've always been the fat friend too!" in the process of writing this book makes me certain these stories or versions of them have been experienced by hundreds or thousands or maybe even hundreds of thousands of girls and women all over the world. But when I was going through them I felt alone, like I was the only one in the world who felt this way. Like I was the only person on the planet who was fatter and less desirable than her friends. I felt like I was the only one, like no one else could possibly understand what I was going through.

That's why I wrote this book. To let you know you're not alone. That the feelings and emotions you feel, whether you are the fat friend or not, are real and valid. To let you know there is someone out there who is going through or has gone through the exact same thing you are going through right now. Because sometimes you just need to know it's not just you, and you aren't the only person in the world who feels that way.

I also wrote this book to let you know there is a way to the other side of every negative and awful thing you have experienced as the fat friend or just a regular girl trying to survive high school or a 30-year-old woman who is still trying to figure out how to navigate all the confusing messages on social media. The dark and dreary reality you are currently living in doesn't have to last forever. There is a light at the end of the tunnel, or even better, there is a light inside that's ready for you to let it out and shine. Confidence, body acceptance, and even self-love are hard work. I can't promise you finding that light will be easy, but I can promise you it will be worth it. As you'll read in the pages ahead, my journey isn't over. I still struggle, sometimes daily, with some of these things. I'm still fighting the fight right alongside you.

I also don't think the struggles and thoughts and ideas I have written here are only dealt with and felt by fat people. I have no doubt there are naturally thin people who will be able to relate to every story I'm about to tell. Conversely, I know there are fat people who have had confidence and an I-don't-give-a-damn attitude from day one, and they may read these words and wonder what the hell is wrong with me. This book isn't for them. This book is for every person who has ever wondered if they'll ever be loved, or if they are even worthy of love. This book is for every person who has cried themselves to sleep at night and prayed with everything they had to be skinny just so the pain would finally stop. This book is for every person who has felt alone, who has had their body shamed, or who has been called fat. This book is for every person who has felt like the fat friend, regardless of body size.

I never thought it would be possible to love myself. I never thought I would be able to like, much less love, my body. You'll hear me talk a lot about my body positivity journey in the coming chapters and how it has made my life infinitely better. I wrote this book because I believe that is achievable for everyone, and I hope by sharing my experiences I can maybe change the heart and mind of even one lonely, heartbroken girl.

These chapters are ordered in a way that makes sense to me, but they can really be read in any order. Each confession is its own, self-contained personal essay. While I hope you'll read it from start to finish, you can also pick and choose the ones that resonate with you and leave the rest. I hope you enjoy.

CONFESSION 1

I AM EMBARRASSED BY MY BODY

I am embarrassed by my body. I am embarrassed and ashamed of my own body.

I am embarrassed by my fat rolls, my thighs that rub together and make holes in my pants, and my big feet. I'm embarrassed by the varicose veins and cellulite on my legs and the fact that my knees are already shit even though I'm only 31. I'm embarrassed by the fact that sometimes my stomach sticks out farther than my boobs and by my B belly. I'm embarrassed that the doctors had to tape my stomach out of the way when I had a C-section to bring my second baby into the world, and I'm embarrassed that sometimes I get the equivalent of diaper rash in between my fat rolls or under my boobs. I'm embarrassed that my arms jiggle when I dance or wave. I'm embarrassed by my double chin and fingers that sometimes look like sausages.

I'm embarrassed that sometimes my body doesn't fit in certain places. I'm embarrassed when I go shopping and think something looks like it will fit only to have to nearly rip the shirt in half to get it back off again. I'm embarrassed that sometimes when I wear a skirt or dress my thighs literally slap together and sound like someone is clapping. I'm embarrassed by the stretch marks that cover my belly and the tops of my breasts, not from having babies, but from gaining a lot of weight really fast when I was in college. I'm embarrassed that no hotel towel in history has ever been able to wrap around even half of my body. I'm embarrassed by the fact that entire clothing brands don't make any clothes in my size and that I have to shop at specialty stores to find things that fit.

I could go on for several more paragraphs, but the point is, I'm embarrassed by all of it. I hate looking at it, I hate talking about it, I hate admitting to you that I'm embarrassed by it, and I hate feeling like no one will ever understand. I hate that we don't talk about these things, so we all feel so damn alone.

It wasn't always this way. When I was in elementary school, a few of my friends and I would strip down to our underwear and dance around like belly dancers. Even then my body was much bigger than theirs, but I wasn't embarrassed by it. But somewhere along the way, it changed. I learned that not only was my body type undesirable, it was disgusting and I should keep it hidden. Somewhere along the way, I learned to be embarrassed and ashamed of my body because it didn't look like everyone else's.

Maybe it was because the boys in my high school used to make fun of how big my butt looked in the white shorts of my basketball uniform. Maybe it's because every other person on my volleyball team had a flat stomach when they took off their uniforms. Maybe it's because I got called a fat-ass more than once by boys I thought I had crushes on. Maybe it's all of that and more, but whatever the reason, I learned to be ashamed of my body, and it's something that has stayed with me.

When I was in high school, I mastered the art of changing in open locker rooms without ever showing my stomach. I used to be proud of the fact that I could change out of a sweaty sports bra into a regular one on a moving school bus without ever taking my shirt off because God forbid anyone see my stomach and fat rolls. When I was in situations where I needed to fully change, I always used a bathroom stall.

The embarrassment of my body continued well into my adult life. There was the time I lost my panties in a guy's bedroom and had to turn the light on to find them. Never mind that we'd both been naked two minutes before, those moments with the light on were humiliating. I also distinctly remember the first time I got an ultrasound when I was pregnant with my first baby and was asked to lift up my stomach so they could get a better view. It made me want to cry. I might have even cried in the car after the appointment. I didn't have a cute, round bump that protruded out from my pubic bone. Instead, I had a big, disgusting fat roll I had to move out of the way to be able to see my baby on an ultrasound.

My belly continues to torment me to this day. I knew I was having a C-section before my second baby was born. I did all the research. I knew they would have to move my belly out of the way. But that still didn't prepare me for the shame I felt, lying there on the operating room table half-naked, while the nurses ran around trying to find the right sticky tape to hold my stomach up. It didn't prepare me for how gross it would make me feel to have them pull my stomach up tight and secure it with a big, medical-grade adhesive pad.

When people would tell me to make sure I had granny panties so my regular ones didn't hit my C-section scar after the birth, I was too embarrassed to tell them my panties have never hit that part of my stomach because of my fat roll. I was too embarrassed to tell them I was way more concerned about keeping my scar dry and clean down there in the folds of fat and skin so it didn't get an infection. I was never worried about the "C-section shelf" you hear about sometimes because I already had that, except most people just call it a fat roll.

The shame and embarrassment I have felt for my body through the years is one of the things that has felt most isolating. I know everyone struggles with body image from time to time and lets comments made by jerk boys hurt their feelings. I know all sorts of people, even skinny ones, deal with binge-eating and feeling out of control around food. But I don't know any other people with half the things I listed above because we don't talk about it. I don't know anyone else with a B belly or anyone who had to have their stomach taped out of the way during a C-section. I don't know anyone else who repeatedly rubs holes in the thighs of their pants.

Sometimes just knowing someone else is going through the exact same thing you are makes the burden a little easier to carry. Sometimes knowing someone else is struggling just as hard as you are makes everything seem a little better because at least you know you are not alone in the fight. Sometimes knowing someone else has gross varicose veins at age 30 would make me feel better about mine.

Practicing self-love and body positivity has helped me come a long way in regard to the embarrassment I've felt over the years. I have learned to stop feeling ashamed by some of those "embarrassments," but some of them still make feel like that same 17-year-old girl changing bras under her shirt so no one would see her. I have come across a lot of people who have the exact same body image issues and feelings of worthlessness that I do, but in some regard, I feel just as alone as I ever have because it seems like no one else has the same things to be embarrassed about as I do.

I am 100 percent certain that I am not the only person who has some or all of those things, but I don't know for sure because we are all too embarrassed to talk about it. Even I, a self-proclaimed body positivity advocate, don't talk about all these "flaws" (until now) and why I'm so embarrassed by them. I will talk all day about how loving myself changed my life and how I still have really hard days when it comes to being positive about my body, but talk about the shame I still feel for certain parts of my body? Show those parts to the world? No way. That would be too real.

Despite my own embarrassment, I think the only way any of us are going to get over it and stop being ashamed of our own bodies is by talking about it. We have to open up the dialogue and be vulnerable together. How is anyone supposed to know it's okay to be 31 and not be able to drop it like it's hot because of bad knees if we don't say it out loud? How is anyone supposed to know that other people rub holes in the thighs of their pants too? How are we supposed to know that we are all flawed, imperfect human beings with things we are embarrassed about if no one ever admits it?

It's amazing the response I get whenever I talk about my insecurities on social media. People always comment about how they feel the same way or they share their own insecurities. People are vulnerable and real, all because me talking about my issues gives them permission to talk about theirs too. It's a really beautiful thing.

We have to talk about all the perceived flaws, all the insecurities, and all the raw emotions we feel as humans so we can connect with others who feel the same way and stop feeling so damn alone. We have to talk about all the things we are embarrassed by and untangle the web of lies that has led us to be so ashamed in the first place. We have to talk about all the things so maybe one day, we can all realize there is nothing to be embarrassed about after all.

CONFESSION 2

THE LACK OF CLOTHING OPTIONS IS INFURIATING

For once in my life, I want to click on a Facebook or Instagram advertisement for some cute clothes and find something other than small through large options. Is that so much to ask? Apparently, it is. Despite having heard over and over again that the majority of women in the United States are a size 14 and over, I continue to see brand after brand of clothing with limited sizing options, and it is infuriating.

There are whole clothing brands that exclude a huge segment of the population. I went into Lululemon with some friends recently (I had never been to one before) and quickly realized they only carry up to a size 12. Never at any point in my adult life have I been able to wear a size 12, regardless of how stretchy the leggings are. Despite claiming to be body positive, Lululemon doesn't have clothing to fit anything other than the smallest in the population. Hello people, fat girls want to look cute too!

When I was pregnant (meaning hormonal and easily pissed off), I made it my personal mission to comment on every single Facebook ad selling clothing without plus-sized options to let them know it would be really nice if someone would remember fat people get pregnant too and need options for clothing to wear. But pregnancy and all its uncomfortableness, I mean joys, is a topic for another chapter. I'm not the only one who leaves angry comments on Facebook ads. Whenever I scroll through the comments, I inevitably see the request for a larger range of sizes, and the answer from the company is almost always the same: they have heard the comments and are working on expanding their size range. Why is it so hard to launch a product line with more sizes than small, medium, and large? Why can't we start with a full, inclusive range of sizes instead of making it seem like anyone larger than a size 12 is just an afterthought?

I just want to look cute and stylish AND feel comfortable in the clothes I'm wearing. This means I shop almost exclusively at stores and for brands I know cater to plus-sized women. This also means my clothing choices are limited. I can count on one hand the number of stores online or in person I KNOW carry clothing that is going to fit me. That's less than a handful of stores I can confidently order from or walk into and know I won't have an issue finding clothes. At the mall closest to my home, there is only one store in the entire mall on that short list. That is one of the 35 women's clothing stores listed in the mall's directory where I can comfortably shop. That is only 3 percent! If I add in the stores I'm fairly certain I could find clothing in, it rises to 14 percent. A quick Google search confirmed what I've heard countless times before: over 60 percent of women in the U.S. wear a size 14 or above. I might not be as good at math as I used to be, but I definitely know those numbers don't make sense.

Come on, fashion industry! This is 2019. Fat people exist, and we want clothes to wear. Clothes that aren't ill-fitting, tent-like shirts or dresses and super-stretchy-but not-really-designed-for-curves pants and skirts. I want clothes in colors other than black, in styles made for my body—not just extra fabric added to designs made for skinny people—and I want to be able to find them in stores where my friends shop and in advertisements I see on Instagram. I want to be able to ask someone where they got something or see clothing recommendations from people on Facebook and actually be able to go find that item in my size, and not because I somehow managed to lose four dress sizes.

For years and years, I tried to shop at "normal" clothing stores. It usually did not end well. I clearly remember buying shirts from Aeropostale when I was in high school because I wanted to be like my friends, only to have my volleyball coach pull me aside and tell me I couldn't wear them on bus trips anymore because my stomach was exposed every time I moved.

In college, I bought a $60 pair of ballet flats that were too small because they were the only thing I could squeeze into at a trendy store my roommate shopped at, and I wanted to be able to shop there too. I bought a dress at Nordstrom for the same reason. I spent $80 dollars on it and wore it twice. For many women, clothing is a connector. It's easy to talk about and is a way to show off our personalities and individuality, but when you are a poor, plus-sized college student with limited options for clothes, it can feel like something that sets you apart, and not in a good way. It's really difficult to have a good time when you are constantly worried about how your clothes fit. It's also a really big bummer when someone asks you where you got an item of clothing and you have to name a store they've never even heard of because they aren't fat.

I was 28 or 29 before I really figured out my own sense of style and what types of clothing fit and flatter my body the best. That meant

I spent all of high school, college, and much of the first part of my life as a real adult never feeling comfortable in my clothing. In part, this was because it was so damn hard to find fitted clothes I could afford. At that time, all the plus-sized clothing brands I was aware of were well out of my college-budget price range. How I looked in something or how something fit was always at the forefront of my mind. Questions like "Can you see my fat rolls in this shirt? Are my arms too big for a sleeveless top? Do these jeans make my muffin top even bigger? Is this skirt showing too much of the cellulite on my thighs?" were constantly floating through my head.

All I wanted (and still want) was to be able to find reasonably-priced clothing that fit my body and looked like the styles everyone else was wearing at the time. I used to try and be trendy with the clothes I wore in an effort to fit in, but more often than not they didn't fit well or look good. It is almost impossible to feel good about your body in ill-fitting clothing. Trust me, I've tried. There is a picture of me from my first day of school my junior year of high school that makes me cringe now. I had huge blonde streaks in my hair and was wearing a pair of light wash denim jeans and a green Roxy shirt that was at least one size too small. There was absolutely nothing about that outfit that looked good, and I'm pretty certain I wasn't comfortable in it. I wanted more than anything to be able to wear the same brands and the same types of clothes as my peers, and even the biggest size at those stores was a little too tight, but I bought them anyway because the drive to fit in and "be cool" was a powerful motivator.

I want to be able to walk into the majority of stores and find something that fits me well. I want us to stop labeling brands as "size inclusive" just because they carry a XXL that is the equivalent of a size 16/18. I want brands that carry clothing up to size 24 to stop saying they have styles for "every" body because, news flash, there are plenty of bodies out there bigger than a 24.

I want clothes in bigger sizes to be lumped in with all the rest of the clothes instead of in their own "extended size" section that has a fraction of the number of items as the regular-sized section. I want the plus-size version of clothing to be available in the same fun patterns, prints, and colors as the straight-size version. I want fashion designers and stores to stop ignoring the fact that more women are a size 14 than a size 4 and start making affordable clothes that actually fit a full range of sizes. I want to be able to go shopping with my girlfriends and know I'll also be able to find something other than a purse or scarf without having to go to a specialty store.

I've finally stopped trying to force my body into clothes that don't fit and have embraced the fact that I am plus-sized and probably will be for the rest of my life. I've learned what fits my body and worry less about being "trendy" than I did when I was younger. I've also matured past the point of worrying about what other people think of my clothing or if I'm wearing the right brand. Regardless of being more comfortable in my clothing choices than I have ever been in my life, I still find the lack of clothing options so incredibly frustrating.

For the most part, I have learned to embrace my curves and all the qualities that make me uniquely me, but when it comes to clothing and shopping, I just want to be like everyone else.

CONFESSION 3

IT MAKES ME WANT TO CRY WHEN YOU CALL CELEBRITIES FAT

Whenever I go grocery shopping, at least one of the tabloids in the checkout line has a headline about how fat some random celebrity has gotten or how they've let themselves go. From tiny Christina Aguilera to Kirstie Alley, I swear I've seen every female celebrity be called fat at one point or another. If she's fat, what does that make me? If all you can talk about is how much weight Kelly Clarkson has gained or how skinny Jessica Simpson used to be, I don't even want to know what you think about me.

It's not just tabloids and "critics," though. It seems everyone loves talking about how fat celebrities are, and it makes me want to cry. One day several years ago, my two little sisters and I were at our parents' house watching CMT, and Lady Antebellum was on the TV. The lead singer, Hillary Scott, had recently gained some weight (I actually think she was pregnant, but that is beside the point). My two sisters spent several minutes commenting on her appearance and how much weight she'd gained and how fat she looked. It wasn't just a passing comment or two, it was a full-blown conversation about her weight.

I sat there nearly in tears. If they thought this beautiful woman on the TV in front of me was fat, what on earth did they think about me? So, in a moment of bravery, I asked them.

"If she's fat, what does that make me?"

They backpedaled so fast, I actually find it funny now.

"You're not fat, Paige!"

"That's not what we meant."

"You look great!"

Yeah, okay, like I was going to believe any of that after what I'd heard them say three seconds ago.

It didn't matter that those comments weren't directed at me, they still hurt. I can guarantee you, even at my smallest, I was fatter than Hillary Scott has ever been. If she wasn't pretty enough or skinny enough, then I definitely wasn't.

How could it be that there was this beautiful, accomplished woman on TV, and yet the most interesting thing we could find to talk about was her body? It didn't matter that she had a killer voice and a successful music career because all they were talking about was her weight. If selling millions of albums, being on TV, and selling out concerts across the nation weren't good enough reasons to talk about Hillary Scott instead of focusing on her body size, then I was definitely never going to do anything with my life that would outshine being fat.

There have been dozens of other times similar conversations have played out in front of me when I wasn't brave enough to say anything. Times when I didn't have the courage to call my friends or family out on their ignorance. Times when I've listened to the comments made about celebrities' bodies and then cried myself to sleep later that night because I was never going to measure up to the impossible standards the world has set for women's bodies. Because if the people I knew best thought those celebrities were fat and ugly, then surely they thought the same thing about me.

I've heard and read hundreds of comments about celebrities and their bodies. Everything from the Internet going crazy about Lady Gaga's pooch during her amazing Super Bowl halftime performance in 2017, to designers refusing to make size 8 Bebe Rexa a dress for the Grammys in 2019 because she is too big, to talk about the Kardashians and their big butts. If a celebrity gains weight, it is plastered all over the tabloids and haters come out in droves talking about how disgusting they are. When they lose weight, they are praised for "bouncing back" from pregnancy or interviewed about "how they got their body back."

Have you ever noticed how we don't talk about men's bodies nearly as much as we talk about women's? I've rarely seen hateful comments directed toward men because they are "fat and disgusting." I've rarely seen a man make a tabloid cover because he gained a few pounds. Somewhere along the line, we decided women's bodies were the most important and interesting thing about them. Meanwhile, we are celebrating men's actual accomplishments instead of basing their entire worth and popularity on just how good their bodies look.

All this talk about people we are never going to meet might seem innocent. After all, they are celebrities who choose to live their lives in the spotlight, so in turn, they get our scrutiny and opinions about their bodies. I'm fairly certain most of them couldn't care less what strangers on the Internet have to say about their bodies; that they aren't bothered by and rarely even see or hear the comments from us common folk. But you know who does hear those comments? Me, every person you know who has ever struggled with weight or self-esteem, and little girls who are learning about body image and worthiness from social media and our ignorant comments.

I am not innocent when it comes to this. I, too, have spent more time than I should talking about celebrities' bodies and making rude, sweeping judgments about people I will never know. By doing that, we are perpetuating a toxic culture that only celebrates skinny people and bases worth on body size, and in the process, we are teaching little girls to hate their bodies because they aren't perfect. We are setting up a whole new generation of girls to struggle with body image and self-esteem just like we have, and we don't even realize it. We are making our families and friends feel insecure and unworthy in the body they are in right now because it doesn't look nearly as good as the one you are currently tearing apart.

I know there are people out there who will say we should all be less sensitive and not take comments made about other people so personally. Those people can go to hell. Why don't you try telling a third-grader who is bullied because of her looks not to be so sensitive? I have learned through years of practicing self-love and slowly realizing my body is worthy just the way it is to tune out some of those ignorant comments. To not let opinions about someone else's body ruin my day or my confidence. But for every person out there who has learned self-love, there are dozens more still struggling to accept their bodies, still hating everything they see when they look in the mirror, and still struggling to disregard hateful comments, even if they aren't about them.

I want to cry for all the girls growing up in this age of social media. When I was a little girl, I only had to deal with the mean things people were willing to say to my face. Now, people hide behind their computer screens and fake profiles and hurl insults at people they don't know, and it is so sad. When all we do is critique a woman's appearance, regardless of what other amazing talents she may have, we send the message that looks are all that matter; that unless you look a certain way, nothing else you ever do will be enough. It is a message little girls are getting loud and clear. Is that the message you want to send to your daughters? Your sisters? Your friends?

I don't have a daughter, but I can guarantee you if I did, those are not the things I would want her to learn about self-worth and body image. I would want her to know that she's beautiful no matter what, that beauty goes deeper than the surface, that there are more important things than thigh gaps and the size of jeans she wears, that her successes and failures in life do not hinge on her looks, that she is worth more than the opinions of ignorant people, and that the number of likes she gets on social media don't equal happiness. Most importantly, that she is loved and cherished and worthy whether she's a size 2 or a size 22.

I'm definitely not perfect when it comes to this, but I am trying. The last thing I want to do is make someone else cry themselves to sleep at night because I know that kind of pain, and I wouldn't wish it on anyone. I'm working hard to not comment on anyone's body, celebrity or otherwise, because I am no longer okay with perpetuating the lie that our bodies are the most interesting thing about us. I don't want any part in spreading the message that in order to be worthy of love and respect, you have to look a certain way. Instead, I want to spread a message of love, worthiness, and acceptance because everyone, even celebrities, deserves that.

CONFESSION 4

I WANT TO BE A 10

The whole conversation was demeaning. I would have been disgusted if they were talking about my sister or niece or friend. I should've been appalled, or at the very least defended the girls I'd just spent the last four hours dancing and drinking with, but all I could think was, "I want someone to talk about me like that."

Let me back up and start from the beginning.

I was on vacation visiting one of our good friends with my husband, my toddler was safe with his nana, my first romance book just released, and I had lost 100 pounds in the last year and a half. I was wearing clothing in sizes I hadn't worn in years, and I'd recently discovered how much I loved lipstick. I looked good and felt good. I was rocking a level of confidence I don't think I'd ever felt before. I drank margaritas and ate tacos, played virtual golf, and didn't have a care in the world. I felt like I was on top of the world until that conversation.

It was day two of our little weekend getaway. A day in which I had eaten pancakes and bacon and a hamburger with French fries and didn't even worry about it. We had all been to a soccer game and then went to a local piano bar to meet up with a girl our friend knew and her cousin. We drank fruity cocktails and shots that tasted like pineapple upside-down cake, danced until we were sweaty, and walked the few blocks to a late night pizza place where you can get a slice of pizza as a big as your face for three dollars. I had loved every minute of it. For one of the first times in a long time, worries about my body and how it looked were nowhere to be found.

We parted ways with our new friends, and the three of us went home. I went to the bathroom to get ready for bed, and the guys stayed in the living room to drink beer and talk. I don't think they even knew I could hear them, but I heard every word they were saying. Words like *10* and *hot* and *bang*. They were talking about the girls we had just been hanging out with. One of them would say how hot they were, and the other would agree, and it went back and forth for what felt like a million years. They went on and on about how the girls were "10s" and other things I'll leave to your imagination.

In my still semi-drunk state, I almost started crying. I stood there and looked at myself in the mirror. Looked at my soccer jersey that was a size smaller than the one I wore the year before and the jeans that were the smallest size I'd worn in years; the exact same outfit I had felt confident and skinny in several hours before. I couldn't help but wonder what number they thought I was. I wondered if anyone had ever talked about me like that and if anyone had ever called me a 10. *"Who are you kidding, Paige? Of course no one has,"* I thought to myself.

It didn't matter that one of them was my husband, that he had chosen me over everyone else, that it was my butt he had grabbed all night, or that I was the one he came home to day after day. At that moment, all I wanted was to be those girls.

They ate giant pieces of pizza and drank 1,000 calories of fruity drinks and shots just like I did, but they still looked amazeballs in their tiny dresses. I would be willing to bet it wasn't the first time they had been called 10s, and it probably wasn't going to be the last. And here I was, positive that no one had ever called me a 10 and almost certain that I was probably referred to as the DUFF (designated ugly fat friend, defined by the Urban Dictionary as *Two hot chicks at a bar will have a really nasty fat ugly b*&@h hanging out with them, referred to as a "DUFF"*).

I should probably mention that this was about a year into my self-love journey. I was at a point in my life where I had finally developed some self-confidence and didn't hate my body with every fiber of my being, but it didn't keep the comments of two drunk idiots (I say idiots with as much love as I can because I'm still married to one of them and good friends with the other) from destroying every ounce of self-confidence I had built up. I let a conversation that wasn't even meant for my ears to hurl me back into the darkness of hating my body and myself.

I know that what constitutes a "10" is subjective. I know my husband is attracted to me. I know there is so much more to me than just my body. I know I shouldn't want to be an object to be lusted after. Sitting here, years later, it is easy to see all the rational thoughts I probably should've had back then. It is easy to see how silly and dramatic I was being.

But it was so easy to get sucked into that place because, from the time I was a little girl, my idea of what was considered attractive by society was based on the way women's bodies were portrayed in magazines, on TV, and in advertisements; on the girls at my high school who got dates and the ones who didn't (raising my hand over here); on the types of women who got the most attention from men. I did not and still do not fall into that category of attractive.

It wasn't the first and, unfortunately, probably won't be the last time I will want to be described as a number that has no bearing on my worth as a human being. It won't be the last time I'll want to be the object of someone's desires or will let the demeaning comments of others determine how I feel about myself.

I am more than a little ashamed to admit how much power I have let men—including their oftentimes narrow opinion of what is considered attractive—have over me and the thoughts I have about myself. Never once have I heard a man say, "Damn, check out that girl," about someone who looks like me. I've never once heard them comment on how hot someone even remotely close to my size is. I've let it bother me; let it make me hate my body for years and years. A few months of self-love and body positivity did nothing to shield me from those old feelings resurfacing.

I'd like to think if I was in the same situation now, I wouldn't let those words bother me, but the truth is I'm not sure I'm strong enough to ignore them just yet. As much progress as I have made with those kinds of negative thoughts and feelings and self-talk, I still struggle with those emotions. I still struggle with wanting to be validated and praised for the way I look and still want to be seen as someone physically desirable. I still get jealous when those same two lovable idiots talk about women like they are nothing more than objects on display (after I reprimand them for being pigs, of course). I think if I overheard that same conversation, I'd go to the same dark place and question my worth based on comments that weren't even made about me because confidence and self-love are things I have to fight for every single day, and some days the darkness still wins.

More often than not, I can turn that ship around. I can remind myself of all the reasons why I am desirable that have nothing to do with my body. I can look in the mirror and see the parts of me that I do love and know that regardless of the number someone assigned me, I am beautiful and worthy and loved. I can now see my own way out of that darkness, or I have a few good friends who can remind me when I'm too deep in the black hole to remember.

That night, however, there was no coming back from that dark place. I finished getting ready for bed, kissed my husband good night with tears in my eyes, and fell asleep still wondering what number I was.

Before then, I naively thought I had reached a place where confidence and self-love were plentiful, but in the days following, I realized I hadn't made nearly as much progress as I had thought. Sure, it was easy to love myself at home where my two-year-old told me I was pretty and there was no one to compare myself to, but out in the world where it seemed like every person I met was skinnier or prettier than me, it was harder.

For a few brief, ignorant moments before that night, I thought maybe my struggles with self-esteem and body image were over. I had figured out how to love myself, and now I was going to be confident and untouchable and life would be amazing. Oh, I was so wrong. Not only was my journey not over, it was really just beginning.

Because in the two years since that night I gained 15 pounds, got pregnant, and gained another 60. After I had the baby, I lost 30 of those pounds, only to gain 15 of them back again (thanks to Christmas cookies). It is the same rollercoaster of weight loss/weight gain I have been on my entire life, but this time my newfound self-love and confidence have been tested. Would I still be able to love my body even though it wasn't the same as the one I learned to love a few years before? Would I still be able to love my body even though my damn pre-pregnancy jeans still only come halfway up my thighs? Would I be able to go out and be surrounded by girls that were skinnier or prettier than me and not let my differences make me insecure?

The answers to those questions are a lot more complicated than just yes or no. A few months after my second baby was born, I went on another vacation with my husband and our same friend from before. We were going to Boston for a Patriots football game and I couldn't have been more excited...until I had to pack. I tried on literally every shirt in my closet, and that is not a small number of shirts. I sent my best friend at least a dozen texts trying to figure out which outfits looked the sexiest (yes, I am rolling my eyes at myself as I write this) and then cried in a pile of clothes on my bed when I determined that not only did I not have any outfits that were sexy, but my body just wasn't sexy.

Since I had wasted the entire time I should've been packing trying on clothes, I ended up sending my husband to Target the next morning to pick up the new sweater I had bought in an attempt to find something attractive and warm to wear. Meanwhile, I packed a push-up bra, my brand-new black jeans that were three sizes bigger than the last jeans I had bought, and a few other things I knew didn't make me feel like crap. Much to my surprise, I had an amazing time. Maybe it was because I wasn't surrounded by dozens of beautiful women in tiny dresses, but I went out with my husband and our friend and didn't spend the entire trip thinking about how I looked compared to everyone else or worrying about how fat I looked in my outfit. Despite wearing pants much bigger than the ones I had on the night of the "conversation" and still not being totally comfortable in my postpartum body, I had a good time. I didn't let worries about my looks ruin my trip. There were even a few times I felt good about my body and how it looked.

I gained 60 pounds and still had more confidence and self-assurance than I had while standing in the bathroom listening to my husband and our friend talk about two girls I barely knew. It turns out that knowing my worth and how it isn't tied to my jean size made all the difference in how I let other people's opinions impact me. I had spent a year and a half battling negative self-talk, giving my body grace, and being grateful for the amazing things it was capable of as I grew another human life and brought it into the world. I had practiced saying nice, loving things to myself in the mirror instead of hateful ones, and it made a world of difference. For the first time in my life, I saw a light at the end of the tunnel and could actually envision a time and place when I no longer let the judgments of other people make me feel bad about myself.

Don't get me wrong, every now and then I still get focused on being a 10 and wanting that validation and acceptance from an outside source, but I'm slowly getting closer to the light. I'm slowly learning to base my worth and self-confidence on things that really matter, not arbitrary numbers like my jean size, weight, or the random musings of men who have had too much to drink.

CONFESSION 5

I HATED BEING PREGNANT

Most of the time when people talk about hating pregnancy it's because they throw up every day for nine months, have the worst heartburn ever (I had that too!), or experience all sorts of weird symptoms. But I hated pregnancy for an entirely different reason. I hated being pregnant because it didn't look the way I thought it should. I never got a cute, round belly like you always see in maternity photo shoots. I never looked like the pregnant woman I always pictured in my mind, and it made all my insecurities 1,000 times worse.

Before I got pregnant with my first baby, I used to imagine what it would be like. I thought for sure I'd get morning sickness because my mom had it bad, I thought about how cute it would be to see my baby's foot pressing against my stomach, and I thought about how I would look with a round, pregnant belly. It turns out none of those things were ever going to happen to me.

I was well into my first pregnancy (like the third trimester) before I looked even remotely pregnant instead of just really fat, and not looking the part made me hate my body even more. It was just one more way my body had failed me; one more way being fat was ruining everything. Pregnancy and the babies that came from it was an amazing, beautiful gift that I should've been celebrating. I almost didn't even write this chapter because I know there are women out there who would do anything to be pregnant and who I'm sure will hate me for being so superficial about something they long to be. I know there are women who feel like their bodies failed them for a much less shallow reason, and my heart goes out to them, but during my first pregnancy I didn't appreciate any of it.

I didn't take any photos of my "bump" and tried as hard as I could to not be photographed at all during my pregnancy because not only was my belly growing, so was everything else. Because of this, I only have a handful of pictures of myself during my first pregnancy. If my son ever asks to see me when I was pregnant with him, I'll have almost nothing to show him. If anyone told me I looked cute when I was pregnant, I either brushed it off or said thank you while I thought to myself how they were just saying that to be nice because it's not nice to say, "Wow, you look really fat!"

It wasn't until I was pregnant with my second baby that I discovered I have what is referred to as a "B" belly. I think you can probably figure out what that means, but basically, if I stand sideways and you traced my belly, the shape it makes would look like a "B." For some women, pregnancy forces their belly into a "D" shape instead, but that never happened for me, not even during my second pregnancy when I felt I actually looked pregnant for a good portion of the time.

There are so many tips and tricks for "dressing your bump" when you are pregnant, so many clothing lines dedicated just to pregnant women, but none of them are catering to women who don't have traditional pregnant bellies and need a size bigger than an XL. It was just one more way being pregnant reminded me that my body wasn't and isn't fully accepted by society and just one more reason to hate being fat.

I was ashamed every single time I went to my doctor's office and had gained even more weight. My doctor was amazing and never made me feel like I was doing myself or my baby harm, but I didn't start off at a healthy weight, and I gained 60 pounds during that pregnancy. I was at the highest weight I've ever been in my life the day I gave birth to my son. I hated it. Hated everything about the weight I was gaining, the way my body was growing, and the way I didn't look like I "should."

That hatred stole the joy from my first pregnancy. Instead of focusing on and celebrating the life growing inside of me, I was more worried about how my body didn't look the part. It was the day after my due date (my first son was four days overdue), and my husband and I had gone to breakfast and to run a few errands to pass the time. As we walked into Best Buy I asked him, "Do I look pregnant or just really fat?" At 40 weeks and one day pregnant, I was still concerned about how I looked and whether the world thought I was pregnant or just obese.

Three days later, my body helped me bring a nine-pound baby boy into the world with no drugs, and I still didn't appreciate it. I was so deep in a hole of self-hatred that when I looked at some of the photos our doula took shortly after birth, my first thoughts were, "My belly looks disgusting. My face is huge. I look so gross." I wasn't looking at the tears in my husband's eyes as he saw our baby for the first time or the brand-new baby boy who had just made me a mother.

It makes me cry just writing this. It makes me want to go back and slap some sense into myself. It makes me want to grab myself by the shoulders and shout, "Your body is growing a whole new person. It is giving life to a beautiful little boy. It is literally creating a miracle. Stop being so shallow and ridiculous. Stop wasting these precious moments that you will never get back wallowing in self-hatred. Stop hating yourself when there are thousands of women who would kill to be in your shoes."

I am happy to report my second pregnancy went much smoother, thanks in large part to my ongoing self-love and body positivity journey. While I was still super annoyed at the lack of plus-sized (and tall!) maternity clothing, I didn't hate everything about my body. Some days it wasn't easy. I had to intentionally stop myself from the negative self-talk. On multiple occasions, I said out loud to myself, "Paige, stop. You are growing a human life inside you. Give yourself some grace."

When I was early in my second pregnancy (probably 10 or 12 weeks along), I ordered a pair of tall maternity jeans from Old Navy because by the time my belly was big enough to need them, it was going to be the dead of winter, and they were the only store who carried tall jeans in the size I needed. When they arrived they were a little big in my hips and thighs, but I figured my belly would help hold them up when I actually needed to wear them. February rolled around, and I pulled those pants out to put on before work one day. They were so tight in my thighs I couldn't even get them pulled up all the way.

My stupid pants didn't fit because in the eight weeks since I bought them, my thighs had gotten too big. It wasn't even my pregnant belly that was the problem. Whose thighs get that much bigger in two months? I cried the entire way to work that day because I had been determined to make my second pregnancy healthier and to gain less weight, and I was failing miserably. At that moment, it didn't matter how much I loved my body or appreciated the life it was creating, my damn pants still weren't going to fit. I had nothing to wear, and I'd wasted $40 on pants I couldn't return anymore.

I was mad. Mad for buying pants so early, naively thinking they would still fit. Mad that more stores didn't carry tall pants in plus sizes so I had more options for clothes to wear. Mad for eating too much chocolate chip cookie dough ice cream. Mad for not being more diligent in watching what I ate so I didn't gain as much weight. Mad for gaining 15 pounds before I got pregnant in the first place. Mad that my stupid "B" belly still didn't look pregnant. I was mad at everything.

After my cry on the way to work, I felt better. I took a picture of my crying face in the bathroom mirror and made an Instagram post about how learning to love yourself is really hard and sometimes ugly, but I was still trying really hard. Somehow it made me feel better to cry it out and admit that for a few brief moments, I let that same joy-stealing-hatred from my first pregnancy creep back up. It made me feel better to admit that I'm only human and our expectations don't usually match our reality. It made me feel better to have other people admit they struggle too. It still didn't make my pants fit, but it did make me feel less alone.

I've had to practice giving myself that same grace from the day my jeans didn't fit until this very moment. By the time you read this that baby will have turned one, and I still haven't lost the weight. I still don't "have my body back." I still get random stabbing pains in my C-section scar and still have to fight that same self-hatred I felt during my first pregnancy.

If I have learned anything from pregnancy, it's that just like no two bodies are the same, no two people do pregnancy the same. Some people gain no weight, and some gain a lot. Some people have tiny round basketballs under their shirts, and others gain weight everywhere. But none of that really matters. It doesn't matter that I never had a perfectly round, cute belly or that I gained just as much weight in my thighs as I did in my belly. It doesn't matter that I gained 60 pounds both times I was pregnant or that my babies weighed nine pounds instead of seven pounds like average babies. None of those details matter because my body created two little miracles. It took two tiny cells and grew an entire human being twice! No matter what my pregnant body looked like, I can't deny the sheer magic of it.

When I look at my fat rolls in the mirror and think my body has failed me, I can look at my two sons and know that no matter what shortcomings I think I have, my body created them. And when you think about it, it really is a miracle worth celebrating and being grateful for. Not only did my body give me my sons, but pregnancy was one of the catalysts that helped me see how truly amazing our bodies are and how much of a miracle simply being alive is.

On the days I'm feeling particularly bad about myself, I think about all the things my body does without me even thinking about it. I think about my beating heart and brain making connections I'm not even aware of, and I'm amazed. Even when I can't find it in me to love my body, pregnancy has made me learn to appreciate this body and all the amazing things it does. And sometimes that is just enough to keep the darkness at bay.

CONFESSION 6

I KIND OF HATE "PLUS-SIZED" MODELS

That's not really true. I actually LOVE seeing something other than stick-thin models in magazines, on TV, and in advertisements. I even follow a few badass plus-sized models on Instagram because I love them and everything they stand for. You would think that as a person who has been plus-sized for the last 15 years, I would love the revolution of curvier bodies that seem to be cropping up everywhere, but I don't. Not because they aren't beautiful, but because I hate what constitutes a "plus-sized" model. I hate that they are called plus-sized in the first place, and most of all I hate that they still don't look like me.

When I was in college, I was borderline obsessed with *America's Next Top Model*. I once spent an entire Christmas break watching several seasons that were re-airing on TV and tried not to miss a new episode. Like any other reality TV show, it was a glimpse into a fabulous and not-at-all-what-it-seems-like world that I'll never be a part of. I vividly remember the first time they had a plus-sized model in the competition. She was between a size 8 and 10. I was outraged then and am still at least mildly annoyed by it now, even 10 years later. On what planet is a size 10 considered plus-sized? Most stores that cater to plus-sized women don't even carry a size 10, yet these are the bodies that are being used in the ads selling plus-sized clothing. These bodies don't look anything like my truly plus-sized body or the other variations of plus-sized that don't look like me. In the 10 or so years since I watched that season of ANTM, things have gotten better. Maybe not on the actual show (I wouldn't know, I haven't watched it in years) but in real-life advertising.

There are plus-sized models in *Sports Illustrated* and on the cover! I know some people will say we need to stop glorifying women's bodies altogether and stop viewing them as objects. I 100 percent agree with that, but I'll also take progress where I can get it, and a plus-sized model in *Sports Illustrated* (even if it's the fashion industry's definition of plus-sized) is definitely progress.

Several brands have embraced curvier women as their go-to for advertising, and I love it. I love seeing different and unique body types represented not only on social media but in mainstream media as well. I love that more and more brands are using diverse body types in their ad campaigns. But let's not pretend they are "plus-sized" just because they wear a size 12. These women are gorgeous, and I am in no way shaming their bodies because there was a time in my life (and some days even now) when I would've killed to have a body like Ashley Graham. But just because they are curvier and thicker than traditional models doesn't mean they should be the face of the plus-sized industry.

If you want to do an ad campaign for plus-sized women, try showing someone who doesn't have a flat stomach. The majority of plus-sized models I've ever seen still have a flat stomach. Sure, they don't have washboard abs, but when they stand up there is one single plane from just below their boobs to the top of their bikini bottom. I'm never ever going to look like that, at least not without the help of a plastic surgeon. I want to see my body represented. I want to see what that dress is going to look like on someone with a body type similar to mine, not on a plus-sized model who had to have the dress pinned back so it even fits her.

If we are going to embrace the plus-sized body, then let's really embrace it and not just pretend to while still only using models with the "right" kind of curves. Let's see some models with rolls, real ones, and not the kind that every woman on the planet has when they sit down or lean forward. Let's see some stomachs that aren't flat and some cellulite on butts and bodies that don't look like hourglasses. Let's see some stretch marks because even skinny people get those! I am sure that some of the plus-sized models we see in magazines have some of those things, but they are so photoshopped to perfection you would never know it. It drives me crazy.

Plus-sized is something I have been my entire adult life and a good portion of my teenage years. I know what it's like to have to search for clothing and struggle to find items that fit, are flattering, and fit within my budget. I know what it's like to be the only plus-sized girl in my class or at my job. I don't like the term plus-sized being commandeered by models who could probably easily walk into any store in America and find something to fit them. I don't like stores that cater to plus-sized women using models who might be bigger than a traditional model but STILL have a body type that I am never going to be able to achieve.

Of all the things plus-sized models have that bothers me, the most bothersome is the flat stomach. I honestly don't ever remember a time in my life when I had a flat stomach. I've always had a little or not-so-little pooch below my belly button and sometimes above my belly button too. And let me tell you, clothing looks a lot different on you and fits a lot differently when your stomach isn't even remotely close to flat. Things that seem to look universally flattering on a lot of people almost never look good on me because of the way my stomach is shaped. I very rarely, if ever, see a model with a stomach like mine. I know I can't be alone in this.

There are GORGEOUS women out there with a huge range of body types that, in my non-model/fashion-designer opinion, could easily be models for plus-sized clothing lines. For a while, I naively entertained the thought that I could be one of them and spent my days working at Lane Bryant, just waiting for someone from marketing to come to our store in Salt Lake City and take me out of my boring job refolding the same shirt 20 times a day and plop me into an ad campaign. But I digress. My point is, it shouldn't be hard to find actual plus-sized women with different body shapes to be in ad campaigns.

We are slowly inching away from the all-models-should-be-a-size-two mentality, but we are still very much favoring a body type that I still believe a lot of women will never be able to achieve. I don't have anything against the models who are considered plus-sized by the fashion industry, I really don't. I just don't think people who wear sizes 8 to 12 are actually plus-sized, and they certainly don't fully represent the bodies of the women who wear exclusively plus-sized clothing.

I know I should just get over it and accept the fact that advertisers aren't going to put a person with fat rolls and back fat in national ad campaigns, but at the same time I think it's bullshit. Fat people exist, and if the statistics are to be believed, there are more of us than there are skinny people. We have people who love us and find our bodies sexy, even with our fat rolls. Then again, you would never know it by flipping through any magazine at your local grocery store or browsing for clothes online. You would never know there are a whole host of beautiful sizes and shapes and colors of bodies out there by looking at the majority of models in the world. There are definitely exceptions to this. Knixwear, ThirdLove, and the Dove Real Beauty campaign are a few companies doing a great job at using more diverse models in their advertising campaigns, but they are still in the minority.

Shouldn't the fashion and modeling industry be a reflection of the people they are hoping to eventually sell their clothing to? Don't all types of bodies deserve to be celebrated in the way super skinny an perfectly curvy ones are? I certainly think so, and I can only hope we continue to make progress and that models will continue to look more like the customers they are selling to.

I hope 10 or 15 years from now that my nieces will read this book and wonder what in the world I'm talking about (and who Ashley Graham is) because there are all shapes and sizes of models out there in the world. I hope seeing a fat roll or a stretch mark in mainstream advertising in the norm and photoshopping is so last decade. I hope they'll be able to see their body type, whatever that may be, represented by the fashion industry and in a major advertising campaign. I hope they know that all bodies are acceptable, not just because we talk about them, but because we back it up with the bodies we use in magazines, on runways, and on social media.

CONFESSION 7

LIFE AS A BIGGER PERSON CAN BE UNCOMFORTABLE

The number of times in my life I've asked for a seat belt extender on an airplane: one. The number of times I wanted to ask for a seat belt extender but was too embarrassed, so I just sat through the flight with an uncomfortably tight seat belt: at least 10, maybe more.

I was pregnant with my first baby on a six-hour flight to Hawaii, and there was just no way I could sit with the seat belt digging into me for that long, so I quietly asked the flight attendant for a seat belt extender and put it on as discreetly as I could because I was embarrassed. Embarrassed because even though I was pregnant, the seat belt wouldn't fit across my stomach. Embarrassed that I was big enough to need a seat belt extender and what people around me, family included, thought. I've never asked for a seat belt extender again, but I've thought about it. A lot. Even though I would be infinitely more comfortable, I won't ask for a seat belt extender because that would really just be admitting I'm fat, and I don't think I can handle the embarrassment.

Airplanes aren't the only places I have been physically uncomfortable. I have a friend whose home I frequent, and we often sit outside on the patio where the chairs dig into my thighs because they are a little too narrow or I'm a little too wide. It is uncomfortable at best, painful at worst, but I've never said anything to her about it because again, I'm embarrassed.

There are some spaces in this world that just aren't made for bigger bodies like airplane seats, roller coaster rides, chairs at stadiums, some bus seats, most of the tiny chairs wedding venues seem to prefer, just to name a few. But you better believe I am never, ever going to bring it to your attention that I'm uncomfortable because then I might as well just hold up a big sign that says, "I'm Too Fat for This Space." I would rather literally suffer in silence than draw attention to the fact the size of my body is making me uncomfortable. If I don't bring it up, maybe you won't notice that I'm fat and that my body doesn't fit here.

I have a recurring dream of being somewhere I need to escape from (think a cave), and the only exit is a space that is way too small for my body to fit through. I try to get out and always get stuck and have to try to find another way out, but I always wake up before I manage to free myself. I think this is my mind's way of manifesting the fear I have of being in places where the fact that my body is bigger than most people around me is painfully obvious. I think it's my mind's way of saying, *"Hey, Paige, did you forget you are bigger than most of your friends? Don't worry, I'll remind you with dreams of places they can escape and you cannot. You're welcome!"* Our brains are so rude sometimes.

We've already covered the fact that I've always been the biggest person in my friend group, hence the name of this book. You know that, I know that, so why would I want to bring it to the attention of the group so we can all share awkward glances and then change the subject with a fake laugh? If I bring my body size to attention, is everyone going to wonder why I'm eating a cookie instead of trying to lose weight so I can fit in more spaces? Am I going to make other people uncomfortable by telling them I'm uncomfortable? I'd rather just avoid it all.

I'm not even at the bigger end of the fat spectrum and I feel this way. I've never actually been refused a seat on an airplane or asked to buy two seats. Except for when I was nine months pregnant, I've never had to be reseated at a restaurant because I couldn't fit in the booth. I've never had to get off the roller coaster ride because the restraint wouldn't close. I can honestly say I've never been in one of those terribly embarrassing and degrading situations where the fat person has to leave because they won't fit. I can't even imagine what that would feel like, but I've still felt the sting of being too big for certain spaces; the sting of realizing the world doesn't accept and welcome your body the way it is right now. I've internalized that shame and turned it into one more reason why my body isn't good enough, but I do it in silence so no one knows I'm embarrassed and ashamed of my too-big body.

I'm sure there are dozens more places where fat bodies are discriminated against every single day, places that just aren't made for bigger bodies. I know there are bodies out there bigger than mine, that have faced discrimination and dealt with hatred far more often than I have. I know there are bodies that are both bigger and of color that experience injustices I know nothing about. I know there are people with experiences far worse than mine, and my heart breaks for those people because if I feel ashamed and uncomfortable in many situations, how do they feel?

I also know there are people out there who will read this chapter, or maybe even this whole book and think, *"Well, maybe you should lose weight and none of this would be a problem. You wouldn't need a seat belt extender if you'd just exercise once in a while."* I know without a doubt that this is the case because anytime I see a fat person on social media, whether they are embracing their body or complaining about discrimination, there are inevitably comments about losing weight. There are always comments about working out; thanks for the suggestion, we'll all try running now (insert eye roll here). There are always comments with faux concern about the poster's health or the lifestyle they are passing on to their children. Am I supposed to believe a stranger on the Internet is really concerned about my health? Sure, there may be people who really do mean well, but most of the time people hide their fatphobia behind the shield of health. Some people don't even try to hide it and just make plain mean comments, like calling the poster disgusting, fat, and unlovable. If you want an example, Google the plus-sized Nike mannequin and then read some comments. In the spring of 2019, a Nike store in London displayed a plus-sized mannequin in workout gear and the world/Internet literally lost their minds.

Regardless of what Internet trolls have to say, I'm here to tell you every single person on this planet deserves the respect to be able to take up whatever space we need without being ashamed about it. It doesn't matter if you are tall, short, fat, or thin; that respect is something we all deserve. For many years, I tried to take up as little space as possible and tried to shrink my body in every way I could because I have felt that shame of being too big for a space. I have felt the shame of wondering if a chair would hold my weight. I have felt the shame of feeling like I didn't belong because of my size, and it is not a good feeling.

Over the course of the last few years, I have come to realize my body is not an apology. I don't have to cower in shame because my body takes up more space than yours does. I am allowed to take up space. We all are. Bodies of every shape, size, color, and gender deserve to take up space. My body is not less worthy of space because it is bigger than all the people who are smaller than me. Fat bodies are not inherently worse than skinny bodies, and no one deserves to be discriminated against because of their size.

CONFESSION 8

MY LIFE HAS BEEN ONE BIG DIET

I am always in one of two states when it comes to eating: dieting or eating everything without any control. If it's the latter, I feel guilty and immediately diet again. Some people call it yo-yo dieting. I call it life. When it comes to diets, I've tried them all. From the cabbage soup diet, to Weight Watchers, to paleo, to HCG, to custom meal plans created just for me by trainers. If there is a diet out there that doesn't require buying a bunch of premade, prepackaged frozen food, I've tried it.

It started when I was 14. I was in eighth grade and had a burgundy pixie cut (I promise you it looked as awesome as it sounds). The wife of my mom's boss at the time was a personal trainer, and I met with her a few times. I was really excited about it. I couldn't tell you anything I learned from her, other than I could eat Fig Newtons and Tootsie Pops if I needed a treat. But I do know that was just the beginning of my life of dieting.

Before I graduated from high school, I would try the cabbage soup diet and use my grandma's old Weight Watchers books to try that too. In college, I hired a personal trainer from the field house, and while she mostly coached me on exercises, I picked up a few pointers from her and tried eating less. I actually bought Weight Watchers for myself and tried it again.

Shortly after college, I did the HCG diet. You know, the one where you shoot yourself up with synthetic hormones and only eat 500 calories a day? It totally worked for the 21 days I did that, but just like every other diet I tried in the past, the weight always came back, usually with a few extra pounds. So I tried more things. More personal trainers, more supplements, more meal plans I didn't follow very well (if you are mentally adding up the cost of all of this in your head, yes, I know the number is well into the thousands). There have been times I've tried to dress my diet up and make it sound better by saying, "I'm just eating healthier," but that's bullshit. I'm not cutting out ice cream and popcorn just because it's fun and "healthier."

After I had my first baby, I did another 15-day challenge where I ate the same three meals for two weeks and then tried paleo for a short time, but that did not go over well with my husband. I've tried low carb, low fat, and high protein. I've counted calories and points and macros and followed meal plans that required me to cook two different dinners every single night. Keto is probably one of the only fad diets I haven't tried because I love carbs too much. It has been a constant roller coaster of on-the-diet, off-the-diet, on-the-diet, off-the-diet for the past 15 plus years.

All of it has led to incredible shame and guilt when it comes to food. There has always been bad food and good food. There have always been foods I'm supposed to feel guilty for eating and that should be off-limits. Even with as much progress as I have made in other areas of self-love and body positivity and all of that, food is still my biggest weakness. Food is still very much based on emotions. Food is still a way to cope, a way to celebrate, and at the center of a lot of my thoughts. No matter what else is happening in my life, food has always been there as a comfort. Even though somewhere inside me I know all foods can have a place in a well-balanced diet, there are still foods I inherently think of as bad. There are still foods that make me feel guilty when I eat them and foods I binge eat in shame because it's what I've always done.

As much as I've tried, I still can't look at food objectively. That means that most of the time when servers at restaurants ask if I want to see a dessert menu, I usually say no, even when I always want to say yes. It means I eat in secret a lot. It means more than once I've lied to the trainer I was working with about how well I stuck to my plan that week because I didn't want to admit I was a total failure. Who wants to admit that they sucked *again*? Who wants to admit this is the 700th diet they've tried and yet they are still fat? Who wants to admit that food holds that much power over them?

I have said no to foods on a million different occasions because "I can't have that on my diet." More than once, I've said no to going to parties and outings with friends because I was afraid of going off my diet. More than once, I've "messed up" and then binged everything in my house because if I was going to eat one brownie, I might as well eat them all, along with the cereal, the chips, and whatever ice cream products were in my freezer.

More of my life has probably been spent thinking about, tracking, measuring, weighing, and feeling too many emotions about food than any other category of thought. Too much of my life has revolved around dieting and food.

Even now, as I sit here writing this chapter, I have "fallen off the wagon." I am counting macros, or maybe I should say I'm pretending to count macros because I haven't really tracked much all week, and I'm struggling with what I'm going to tell my macro coach at my check-in tomorrow. I actually love counting macros because it gives me so much more flexibility to eat the foods I love and still reach my goals. It is the best and most sustainable way I have found to create and keep healthier habits, but right now I'm in a battle between wanting to lose the rest of the baby weight and wanting to eat without logging it into an app. I'm in a battle between still wanting to make changes to my body, changes that require a stricter diet than I have been following, and wanting to give up dieting forever. I am in a battle for control over food, and right now food is winning.

I have been on the diet rollercoaster ride for almost two decades. Can I get off now? I want to have a healthy relationship with food, but a lifetime of dieting and restriction and labeling certain foods as bad has left me less than confident that it'll ever become a reality. I want to be able to look at food and have no emotional ties to it; no feelings of good or bad or shame, just food. I want to truly not care about how many calories or how much protein a food has in it, but right now that is almost all I think about when it comes to food.

I want to figure out how to eat healthier because I know the positive impact it has on my life, and it has nothing to do with weight. I feel better, have more energy, and even sleep better when I'm eating more fruits and vegetables and less sugar. But because I grew up inundated with the toxic messages of diet culture, I don't know how to do that in a non-diet way or in a way that doesn't lead to guilt when I do indulge in a sweet treat. I don't know how to unravel my emotions and biases that are so tightly wound around food.

It's amazing watching my son eat. He eats when he's hungry and stops when he's full. Even when it comes to things like ice cream, he eventually loses interest when he's satisfied and moves on with his day. He is the definition of an intuitive eater. I'm trying really hard not to mess that up because I truly believe we were all born like that. Born knowing how to listen to our bodies and our hunger cues, and born without emotional ties to food. But somewhere along the way, diet culture ruined everything. We learned to label foods good or bad, and we learned to feel shame when we ate bad food or overate. We learned all the rules and stopped trusting ourselves along the way.

How would it feel as a fat person to not be on a diet? How would it feel to really and truly just accept that maybe this is a size I am going to be for the rest of my life? How would it feel to once and for all ditch the diet and eat without shame? How would it feel to eat to fuel my body in the best way possible, but not feel guilty about indulgences? How would it feel to cut the emotional ties and have an objective relationship with food? How would it feel to no longer have to fight against the power food holds over me? How would it feel to just eat without thinking about calories or macros or if the food is off plan?

I don't know the answers to these questions, but I hope one day I'll be able to find out. While I can say I love myself and my body as it is right now, I haven't yet made peace with the idea of never losing weight again or with having to throw out all the pre-pregnancy clothes I still have in my closet. Even though I have found some self-love, I am still working toward being a healthier version of myself, and that includes losing some weight.

I'm still working on untangling the web of emotions and thoughts I have about diets, losing weight and being healthy. I'm looking forward to the day when I've finally figured it out.

CONFESSION 9

I HAVE AN IRRATIONAL FEAR OF BEING BIGGER THAN MY PARTNER

Maybe it's because every romantic comedy and every romance novel in history has a scene where the girl is wearing her boyfriend's/husband's/casual hookup's T-shirt or button-down in the morning. Or maybe it's because I was 16 before any boys my age were taller than me. Or maybe I still remember every single mean comment I overheard a classmate make about me in high school insinuating that I was going to marry a tiny person and thinking it was hilarious. Whatever the reason, I have always had a slightly irrational fear of being the bigger person in a romantic relationship.

You aren't taller than me? No, thanks. Does it look like I could pick you up? I'll pass. Is there a possibility I'll squish you when we have sex? Yeah, no. I would like to pretend that means I turned away tons and tons of potential dates and limited myself to a small pool of guys, but let's be real. No one, bigger than me or otherwise, was clamoring for me to be with them. But in my mind, the perfect guy was out there. He was tall, at least 6-foot-3, and athletic; not bodybuilder athletic, but strong and muscular enough to pick me up (after I lost all the weight, of course) and carry me across the threshold after we got married like he was supposed to. I would be able to wear his shirt, and it would be big enough to completely cover my butt like it always did in the movies. Also, there would be no one getting squished in the bedroom.

Back in the real world, that fear meant I obsessed over what my future husband was going to look like. It means I still feel silly if I wear a really short heel and am taller than my actual husband. It means most of the time, my husband doesn't even know how much I weigh because it would be unbearable if I possibly weighed more than he did. It means if I wear his shirt it just looks like a shirt, sometimes a baggy one, but not something sexy that hides just enough of my butt for me to walk around the house and tease him. It means I've wished, more than once, that I was shorter (and skinnier) or my husband was taller just so we could fit some weird Hollywood standard.

This has bothered me to the point where I would get irrationally angry anytime I would see really short girls with super tall guys. I would think to myself, *"Listen, bitches, there are plenty of guys taller than your tiny 5-foot-2 body. There aren't that many guys taller than my 6-foot body, so stay in your own dating pool."* That makes me sound a little bit crazy, I know. But if you are a taller lady, don't tell me you haven't thought the same thing before because I won't believe you.

One of my best friends and I had a conversation about this recently when I was wearing one of the only pairs of shoes I own that have any sort of heel on them. We went to get sushi, and when she complimented my shoes on the way out, I said something like,

"Oh, thanks. I don't wear them very often because then I'm taller than J."

We talked about how Nicole Kidman is a lot taller than Keith Urban and Tom Cruise was quite a bit shorter than Katie Holmes, and as my friend pointed out, it doesn't seem like either of them minded. But my friend also said I'm not the only girl she knows who doesn't wear heels because then they'd be taller than their partner. Maybe celebrities don't care because no one is going to complain when your wife is a super successful actress, or maybe they really don't give a damn because who cares as long as you're happy, right?

Where did this idea that women have to be smaller than their men come from? In medieval times, having a fat wife was considered a sign of wealth and status because it meant you could afford to feed her well. However, somewhere along the way things changed. Maybe it's because men are typically seen as the protector and if a woman is bigger than the man how can he properly protect her? Maybe it all goes back to the misguided idea that in order to be feminine you have to be small and meek. Whatever the reason, it became some sort of unspoken requirement that women be smaller and shorter than their partners.

Much to my disappointment, I'm guilty of perpetuating this idea in my romance novels. Both have at least one scene where the heroine is wearing her lover's clothing and is, of course, looking super sexy in their dirty T-shirt from the day before. Both of them have tall, super fit heroes and curvy-in-all-the-right-places heroines. I know, I'm sorry, I promise I'll do better in my next novel and all the ones after that. This myth, the one where women are only lovable if they are petite and definitely smaller than their lovers, has to be squashed immediately (pun totally intended).

It's not like my husband has ever complained about me being

practically the same size as him, but I still want to be smaller than him. I think some of it has to do with feeling pretty and feminine, and I think a lot of it has to do with the pressures society puts on women. You know the ones where we are supposed to watch our weight and look good so we can one day find a successful husband to take care of us? While we've managed to ditch the part about needing a man to take care of us, we are still clinging to the part where we need to look a certain way to find someone to love us.

I have been married for seven years, and even though I know my husband loves me, I'm *still* holding onto some ridiculous ideal that someone else decided our relationship needed to meet. Why do we (and when I say we, I mostly mean me) do that?

I think a lot of it has to do with the culture we are exposed to over and over again as we grow up. Can you think of a celebrity couple where the woman is markedly bigger than the man? I honestly can't. I can barely think of a non-celebrity couple where the woman is significantly bigger than the man. If all we are shown are couples where the woman fits perfectly into the crook of her man's arm, even in her heels, what else are we supposed to strive for? What else are we supposed to think is normal and acceptable?

I also think at least part of it goes back to confidence. Confidence in myself, confidence in my body, confidence in our relationship. I'm still a newbie when it comes to gaining and keeping confidence. I'm still new at learning to disregard the opinions and standards of others and living my life on my own terms.

Based simply on the number of times my husband slaps my butt or tries to take off my bra in any given day, I can confidently say he doesn't have any issues with my body. He thinks I'm sexy and beautiful and plenty feminine enough. While his appreciation for my body doesn't make me appreciate it more, it needs to be reason enough for me to stop worrying about fitting into someone else's recipe for happiness.

As I've followed more and more body positive influencers on social media, I have become exposed to more bodies and relationships that don't fit the typical mold, and it's awesome. It is refreshing to see people of all shapes, sizes, and colors living their lives and enjoying their relationships without any care what the outside world thinks. And isn't that how it should be? Shouldn't we get to decide what makes our relationship happy or not? Shouldn't we get to decide who we find attractive or who we want to be with and not base our relationships on what social media says is acceptable?

Relationships are hard enough without worrying about living up to "looking the part," and I'm done subjecting my relationship to the pressures of looking like someone else. It doesn't matter if I weigh more or less than my husband because he still tells me I'm beautiful every single day. It doesn't matter if I think I should be shorter because he still loves me. *And I finally believe him.* I believe him when he says I'm pretty or sexy. I believe that he really thinks those things about me, and that is better than fitting any stereotype.

CONFESSION 10

BODY SHAMING OF ANY KIND MAKES ME FURIOUS

It's no secret that fat bodies are shamed, often publicly, and called out for being gross and disgusting, but if you've ever read the comments on a bikini competitor's Instagram post, you know body shaming is not reserved for fat people. People who are deemed to be too skinny are told to eat something, and people who are too fat are told to eat less and work out (like we haven't heard that before). People with small boobs should get big ones, but if your boobs are too big you should get a reduction, and everyone should do the latest glute workout so we can all have round, full butts like the Kardashians. All of it makes me want to throw things across the room.

Curvy bodies are not the only "real" ones. Skinny bodies are not the only ones worth loving. Some people are naturally thin; it doesn't mean they need to eat a hamburger. Some people are naturally larger; it doesn't mean they need to go on a diet. We criticize fat people and tell them to lose weight. We criticize skinny people for being too thin and tell them to gain weight. We tell women they should have round, perky breasts but shame them when they get implants to look how we wanted them to in the first place? Women are supposed to "age gracefully," but don't use Botox or get plastic surgery. It's all a big, confusing double standard that I don't think anyone understands. All I know is there are insults being hurled from every corner of the world about every type of body we can imagine. Can we just stop with the body shaming? All of it.

A while ago, I saw a post on Instagram of a girl who was modeling the different types of bodies that were desirable in different time periods. I assume she had photoshopped herself to showcase how the "perfect" body has changed over time. In the 1400s to 1700s, she was curvy and full-figured, and in the 1920s her body was boyish with very few curves. For the 1950s, she had an exaggerated hourglass figure. She had an extremely skinny body for the 1990s, and for the mid-90s to 2000s she was slim with big boobs and long legs. Right now, the popular look is a super small waist with a big, curvy butt.

The most desirable body type goes through trends, just like clothing fashions, hairstyles, and makeup trends go through cycles. Except unlike those other trends it is simply not possible, without a lot of plastic surgery, for one person to fit every single standard for a "perfect" body as it changes throughout the years. Yet we are still trying to force women to fit the mold of the week. We still shame anyone whose body doesn't fit the ideal of the time, and it makes me furious.

Why do we think we have the right to police other people's bodies? Why do we think it's okay to shame people just because their bodies look different from ours? Why do we believe the lies the diet and beauty industries tell us about what is beautiful and what is not, and then spend billions of dollars a year trying to live up to those lies? Why can't we just mind our own damn business?

As a fat person, I have experienced body shaming in almost every form. Sometimes it's subtle, sometimes it's blatantly obvious, sometimes it's disguised as concern, sometimes it's delivered with outright disdain, but it all hurts. It hurts to have your body called disgusting and viewed as second-class. It hurts to be told no one will ever love you. It hurts to be told you are worthless just because your body is bigger than someone on the Internet deems acceptable.

If you listen to the messages coming from the diet industry, the ideal body shape and size—flat stomachs and hourglass shapes—can be achieved if we work hard enough and follow their program of a strict diet and working out. But that is a lie! Here's the thing about bodies: they are all different. No two people are exactly the same. We are all born with different eye colors, hair colors, heights, skin colors, nose shapes, personalities...the list goes on and on. Why should weight and body shape be any different? Why are we constantly trying to force our bodies into sizes and shapes they weren't meant to be and shaming anyone who can't make it work?

Every person in the world could follow the exact same diet and exercise program, and there would still be a whole range of body types and sizes. There would still be fat people. There would still be super skinny people. There would still be people in the middle.

Nothing illustrates this better than looking at myself and my three sisters. We all grew up in the same household. We were all active and played sports from the time we were young through high school. We ate the same dinners every night growing up and had access to the same food sources outside of the home, yet we are all vastly different. We have all had different shapes from the time we were little girls. Even when we all follow the same diet/exercise plan (which we have done before), our results vary widely because our bodies are not meant to be the same size. Is it any wonder most diets seem to fail in the long run? It's because we are trying to force our bodies to be something they aren't meant to be.

Yet here we are, living in a world where anyone over a size four is too fat. Where Lady Gaga is shamed for having an invisible pooch during her Super Bowl performance instead of being praised for her talent and skill. Where we mask our fatphobia with concerns about people's health. Where everyone, regardless of their shape or size, has probably been body shamed at some point in their lives. Where we all hide behind our keyboards and hurl anonymous insults at people to try and hide our own insecurities. Where the perfect body is constantly changing and we are all just trying to keep up.

For some reason, we have become a culture obsessed with what other people's bodies look like and insist on making sure they know what we think is wrong with them. All that does is perpetuate the idea that only one specific body type is desirable, that we have to look a certain way to be accepted, and that we are worthless if we can't lose the weight and keep it off.

I wish I could say all the bullying and snide comments I have endured in life have made me into a person who never judges other people and their bodies, but I'm almost ashamed to say it hasn't. I don't bully people to their face or on social media, but it doesn't matter. Judging people—whether in my head, out loud in the privacy of my own home, or to friends—is still not okay. I am just as guilty as anyone for making comments, oftentimes rude ones, about people I ignorantly thought were too skinny or super muscular or fatter than me.

I've thought all the same things about people larger than me, things I've wondered my whole life if people were thinking about me. *Maybe if they ate less, they wouldn't be so fat. What kind of clothes would look good on their bodies? Someone that size shouldn't be wearing that.* I've seen people on the street and prayed to God I didn't look that fat and have made weird faces when I've seen a larger woman with a skinny guy. I've mentally corrected people at the gym for doing things wrong and have automatically assumed some bigger people were also unhealthy.

Why? Why would I do that after all the years of dealing with the negative emotions those thoughts and comments from other people have caused me? Why would I knowingly put someone else through all the same things I have suffered through?

The answer to that question, and the reason why all of us shame bodies of every shape and size, is really simple: insecurity. As hard as it is to admit these things, I know I'm not alone. I know I'm not the only one who has these thoughts because I see people on the Internet insulting and judging people they don't know every single day, all because they aren't secure in their own lives and their own confidence. I've seen a quote on social media multiple times that says, "You will never be criticized by someone who is doing more than you. You will only be criticized by someone doing less." It's a simple concept but so powerful.

This is one area where I've been trying really hard to figure out where those thoughts come from. Whenever I make sweeping judgments about other people, whether about their body size or something else entirely, I stop myself and try to figure out why I feel that way. It can be really hard to admit that those thoughts stem from my own insecurities and my own fears of never fitting the mold. Those thoughts come because I'm not confident in myself or my body. As painful as it is to realize, our judgments are usually direct reflections of our own insecurities.

Regardless of where your judgments come from, we have to stop.

There is no such thing as the body police. There is no perfect body. There is no one right way to look, and we aren't accomplishing anything but spreading hate when we shame other people's bodies. My body and how it looks is not your concern, nor is yours mine. We don't all look the same for a reason. Our differences are beautiful, and it's time we start embracing them.

CONFESSION 11

I SAY NO TO GOING OUT TO AVOID BEING THE FAT ONE

Before I developed a little bit of self-confidence and stopped worrying about being the fat friend, I learned lots of ways to cope with the negative feelings that came with being the fattest person in every group. I'd make jokes about myself, was sarcastic and funny, drank too much, and acted loud and obnoxious. But sometimes I just don't want to deal with it. Sometimes I just don't want to be the fat friend anymore.

I was in kindergarten when I started faking sick to get out of class and away from all the situations where I was bigger than my classmates because even in kindergarten, I got made fun of for my size. I spent many hours in elementary school lying on a cot in the nurse's office with a scratchy wool blanket, sometimes sleeping, crying to myself, or thinking about whatever it is seven-year-olds think about.

I remember in first grade I started ballet class with all my friends. We would change into our leotards in the school bathroom and then walk to our dance class across the street. I was an awkward dancer, even back then, and couldn't do a lot of the same things my friends could do. The teacher often pushed me harder than she did my classmates, or at least that's how it seemed to me at the time. I only went for two or three weeks before I told my mom I wanted to quit. I honestly don't remember why my six-year-old self wanted to quit ballet, but I have a strong feeling it was because I felt out of place. A few weeks later when I got tired of having to go home every week when my friends were going to ballet, I asked my mom if I could go again, but she told me no. I had made the choice to quit and had to live with it.

This trend of quitting and faking sick to get out of things I didn't want to do continued until I realized I also didn't get to do the things I actually wanted to do, like play basketball. I stopped faking sick, but I didn't stop finding ways to get out of situations where I was guaranteed to feel awkward.

In college, I was a member of an LDS sorority, and when it came time for the annual fall barn dance and winter formal, I always pretended I had to work. One, because going to either of those events would require me to ask someone out on a date, and two, because I was self-conscious about all the things these group dates would require. I was significantly bigger than all my sorority sisters, I didn't have any cute cowboy clothes or formal wear, and I just didn't want to deal with it.

I made up a ton of excuses over the years as to why I couldn't attend various activities with friends; everything from having to work, to being sick, to pretending I forgot about it until it was too late. I once told a friend that I couldn't do something with her because I had to rearrange the furniture in my studio apartment. If that isn't one of the lamest excuses of all-time, then I don't know what is. I rarely went out to bars with friends because while they were all getting hit on, I would stand in the corner wondering if anyone would ever offer to buy me a drink. I would wonder if they'd have a better time if I wasn't there, taking up too much space and moping.

I know I've missed out on a lot opportunities and fun times, but sometimes it was just easier to stay home than deal with being the fat friend for one more night. Sometimes a pint of ice cream and a *Keeping Up with the Kardashians* or *Sex and the City* marathon made me forget about all the things I could've been doing if I wasn't so damn insecure.

Conversely, when friends didn't invite me to something and I found out about it later, I always wondered if they didn't invite me because I'm fat. Did they leave me out on purpose, or was it just an accident? Have I said no so many times that they've finally just stopped asking? I would wonder every single time I wasn't invited to do something if it was just an oversight or if they didn't want me there because I was too fat or too loud or too obnoxious or too awkward.

None of my friends are bad people. I don't think any of them are intentionally mean, and I can't imagine any situation where they would say, *"Let's not invite Paige tonight because she's too fat."* If your friends do or say things like that, then you need to get new friends immediately. The point is, none of my friends cared about my size. None of them ever purposely tried to leave me out because I was fat, or if they did, I didn't know about it (and still don't want to know about it). I did that to myself. I isolated myself because I didn't know how to deal with my emotions and the shame I created in my head of *always* being the fat friend.

It wasn't even just about my body. I sometimes wondered if all the habits I developed to protect myself were super annoying, if maybe my friends wished I talked less and told fewer stories. Not to mention, it was exhausting to always put on a happy face even when I didn't feel like it, to always play the part of the loud and sarcastic one, and to hold my stomach in all night long so I didn't look as big.

It was easier to just say no, stay home, and mope about how fat I was and how nobody wanted me around, even though the only reason I was home alone was because of myself. No one was excluding me but me. Social situations weren't the only times I projected my feelings on others and then let myself feel bad about them. They weren't the only times I missed out on making memories because I was too busy worrying about my body and what everyone thought about it. Hiding behind my weight and body insecurities was a crutch I used throughout most of my twenties. If I let myself believe that no one wanted me around and they were all disgusted by my body, then I could continue hating myself and feeling like I was never good enough because if my friends felt that way, it gave me permission to feel that way too.

Can I tell you a secret, though? No one else has ever cared about my body or how much space it takes up as much as I do. No one else will ever care as much as I do. No one else will ever even notice half the things I think make me disgusting and unworthy of friends. Real friends couldn't care less what size my jeans are; they just want to hang out with me. And the same thing applies to you.

It took me longer than I would like to admit to realize that using my insecurities as a crutch and an excuse to hide at home was only hurting myself. It took me a while to figure out that once I told my friends no, they weren't out having a terrible time because I wasn't there. They weren't the ones missing out. I was. Being insecure and having no measurable self-confidence wasn't hurting anyone but me. Saying no and faking sick and quitting things didn't impact anyone but me.

I don't regret a lot of things in my life because everything has made me who I am today, but this is one of the things I do regret. I regret all the things I never did because I was too ashamed or scared or busy hiding at home. While I probably didn't miss out on becoming the next great ballerina, I know I missed out on other amazing things. I know I missed out on making memories and living life to the fullest for several years because I was always waiting. Waiting until I lost the weight or until my goal jeans fit or until I was skinnier like my friends. How many things did I miss out on because I kept saying no? I'm certain it's too many to count.

If I could go back in time and give my younger self one message, it would be this: stop saying no, stop quitting, and stop hiding at home because you are tired of being the fat friend. No one gives a damn; literally no one worth having in your life cares. Stop waiting for some magic number on the scale to live your life. Stop putting your dreams on hold because you think everything will magically be better when you lose weight. Live your life right this second, and stop wasting time. This is the only life you get, and the people you love are waiting for you to join them.

CONFESSION 12

I DON'T WANT TO GO SHOPPING WITH YOU, EVER.

W hen I was younger, I used to watch movies or TV shows and see groups of friends shopping together at the mall and think, "That looks fun." I used to think it would be super fun to try on cute outfits while talking about boys and clothes and makeup. Wrong. I was so wrong. There is absolutely nothing fun about going to store after store and pulling the largest size of cute items off the rack, only to realize their XL would have maybe fit me when I was 10. There is nothing fun about trying on clothes that don't fit for hours on end. There is nothing fun about seeing your friends buy item after item of cute clothing when you can't even find one thing.

I didn't grow up where there was a mall and rarely went shopping with anyone other than my mom and sisters because shopping for clothes was usually a whole-day excursion or even a weekend to the city. I vaguely remember one of the first times I went shopping with a group of friends. I was in college, and we went to Nordstrom. I'm pretty sure we were looking for dresses to wear when we went to see a Broadway play in New York City. I struggled to find anything in my size, partly because the store was huge and I had no idea what I was looking for, and partly because I wanted to shop in the same section as my friends. I bought a $80 dress that I couldn't really afford at the time. I wore it a total of two times and packed it from apartment to apartment before I had to resign myself to the fact that it didn't fit anymore and had probably never really fit properly in the first place.

There have been many more shopping experiences since that time. Trips where I tried in vain to find something that would fit from stores like American Eagle and Nordstrom Rack to local boutiques. I would try on shirt after shirt or dress after dress because I knew, even then, I wasn't going to find any pants that would fit me at *those* stores. Sometimes I would show my friends and let them try to convince me something didn't look terrible, but most of the time, I discarded all the clothes that didn't fit in a pile on the floor and tried not to cry. Even shoe stores rarely carried the size 11 I needed, so shoe shopping was out too.

I tried so hard to find things that would fit me that I even got stuck in a dress once. It was at least one size too small and fit firmly in the category of not-showing-anyone, but when I went to take it off, I couldn't get it back over my shoulders. I stood in the dressing room in a panic, thinking about how I was going to have to have one of my friends come in and help me, and how they would see me half-naked. Ripping the dress to get out of it and then having to pay for something I couldn't even wear seemed like a better idea than someone seeing me half-undressed. I eventually calmed down enough to work my way out of the dress without ripping anything or needing help, but it wasn't a good experience. It was just another reminder I was not like my friends. One more reminder that I am the different one. That I'm the one who needs specialty stores or sections to find clothes that fit. That I'm the only one who can't find something to fit in a straight-size clothing store. It all sucked.

There is nothing fun about being reminded over and over again that you are the fat friend. As if I could forget. There is nothing fun about pulling something off a rack and thinking it looks like it will fit, only to realize you are actually fatter than you think you are, and it most definitely does not fit. There is nothing fun about watching your friends try on dozens of amazing clothes and knowing none of it would ever fit you.

For years, I tried really hard to embrace shopping with my friends, but I just couldn't do it. It didn't matter if we were in the biggest Nike store I've ever seen in New York City, in cute shops on the streets of Charleston, or at the local mall in Utah. Shopping with friends or even my sisters, who are also smaller than me, has never been fun. Because of that, I stopped going shopping with people. If someone suggested it as an activity, I would either decline or see if I could suggest something else to do. Now my shopping trips with friends, or really any shopping trips that aren't completed from the comfort of my couch, are few and far between.

I recently, however, had an experience shopping with friends for the first time in years. I started writing this book long before we made plans to go and had this confession already written down as a chapter to write when we decided to go to lunch and then shopping for a girls' day. I had made a lot of progress when it came to my insecurities about clothing since the last time I had gone shopping with friends, but I was still apprehensive. I was curious if it would turn out much the same as it did before with me feeling sad and left out or if I would be able to use my still-in-its-infancy body positivity and self-love to make it a better experience. I thought about this book and this chapter a good portion of the trip. I thought about what I would say and wondered if I would still hate group shopping trips when it was over.

I think it is worth mentioning these aren't just friends I occasionally hang out with. These are some of my best friends; the ones who have regular hours-long Facetime sessions because we can't always get together. These are the friends I have been shopping with most in my adult life and probably have no idea (until they read this) that I hated it.

This most recent shopping trip was infinitely better than those in the past. Though, to be honest, it still bothers me that straight-sized clothing runs the same in most stores, meaning my friends can buy tons of things without ever trying them on and know they'll fit, while plus-sized stores have decided to start labeling clothing weird (news flash: calling it a o when it's really a 14/16 isn't making anyone feel better) and I have to try everything on.

However, I realized something, and it's that I've been missing the point this entire time. Like many other areas of my life, I had been letting my insecurities and self-pity hold me back from having a good time. I finally figured out that shopping with friends doesn't have to be about the actual shopping. It doesn't have to be hours of suffering and hating my too-big body for not fitting into the clothes and cursing the fashion industry for not making plus-sized clothing more readily available.

Shopping with friends can and should be about the experience and time spent with them. It's time that doesn't come around often enough, and it's time I had been wasting because I was too wrapped up in myself to even realize what I was missing out on. It should be about the stories and conversations and laughs we have, not a competition to see who can find the most clothes. It should be about building and nurturing the relationships I have with people I love.

Everything doesn't have to be about body size or the differences between me and any of my friends. In fact, everything shouldn't be about body size and shape because there are so many more things to focus on. There is too much life to be lived, friendships to be nurtured, and laughs to be had to be making the size of my body the focus of anything.

So the next time a friend asks me to go shopping (if any of them ever do after reading this), I'm going to say yes, and not reluctantly. I'm going to focus on having conversations about things other than clothes and on making memories. I'm going to go and worry less about finding clothes I don't need and more on the precious time I get to spend with my friends and the people I love most.

CONFESSION 13

JUST BECAUSE I'M FAT DOESN'T MEAN I'M UNHEALTHY

If you looked at my body, it might not be apparent that I know anything about health and fitness. It might not be apparent that when my sisters or mom start a new workout or diet regime, I'm usually the first one they go to if they have questions. Sometimes when people talk about health and fitness trends, it can sound like they are speaking a foreign language when they mention keto, paleo, macros, carb-cycling, HIIT, intermittent fasting, Tabata, cross-fit, BMI, TDEE, BMR, and dozens of other acronyms and terms that get thrown around everywhere. I have a working knowledge of a lot of it, and I know my way around a gym and free weights. This is partly because I've tried all of it in my quest to lose weight, and partly because health and nutrition and learning are interesting to me. However, from the outside, you would never know it.

I know when I think of healthy and fit people, I think of the trim and toned people you see all over Instagram these days. The ones who actually look good working out in just their sports bras and spandex, and the ones who don't ever have to squish themselves into a pair of jeans because they ate too much pizza the day before. In case you haven't noticed, I am not one of those people. I look like I ate all the pizza and then the ice cream and haven't really worked out any time this decade.

I could easily walk you through the basics of several of the most popular diets, help you calculate your macros should you want to count them, and show you the proper form for dozens of exercises at home and at the gym. If you are in my family or close friend circle, you've probably been corrected by me about health-related things at some point over the years. Anyone who really knows me shouldn't be surprised by this; I'm kind of a know-it-all.

Despite knowing all this stuff, I'm still fat. For a long time, I let that impact my view of myself. Sometimes I still let it. Over the years, I convinced myself that I was a total and complete failure because I had all the knowledge, yet I still couldn't figure out how to get skinny. I had paid trainers and spent thousands and thousands of dollars on programs to teach me how to be healthy, and here I am still medically classified (according to body mass index, or BMI) as obese.

Maybe I'm delusional, but I don't think I really look obese. Fat, sure, but obese isn't a word I associate with myself. If I ever refer to myself as obese, people vehemently disagree with me. Regardless of what I think or what anyone says about me, obese is a word that has been used to describe me at least once.

I am the kind of nerd who looks up medical reports (where available) about myself and reads them, typically before any doctor has even called me with the results. Three and a half years ago, after I was discharged from the hospital for having blood clots in my lungs, I pulled up the discharge report. One of the first few sentences read, "Patient is a 28-year-old obese female." I mean, I know I wasn't exactly skinny at the time. I was only three months out from having my first baby and hadn't lost most of the weight I'd gained during pregnancy yet. In fact, I was actually at the heaviest non-pregnant weight I had ever been, but reading those words in black and white was still a little rough. Obese? Really? They didn't even weigh me the entire time I was in the hospital, so this observation had to have been based solely on how I looked, and according to the doctor writing my report, I looked obese.

I truly felt like a failure at life. Despite all the money and time and effort I had put into being healthy and losing weight over the years, there I was, a 28-year-old new mom being classified as obese. None of my knowledge or know-it-all attitude had been able to prevent me from getting to that place. To say it stung would be a gross understatement. I might have cried at work that day.

I think it is worth noting here how much weight (pun not intended) we give certain words. It's very clear I have a strong negative reaction to the word obese. I have assigned a certain level of shame and stigma to that word, just like many people do with the word fat. I could accept being fat, but being obese made me feel much worse about myself. Just one word and the associations I gave it had the power to make me want to cry in my cubicle. Removing that stigma and shame is a topic for later in the book, but back to the story.

That incident is what motivated me to start really getting healthy and led to the beginning of my body positivity journey. It was less about being called obese and more about being there for my little boy as he grew up and being able to play and run with him. But I would be lying if I said reading that report and feeling the shame at being labeled obese didn't motivate me at least a little.

Since that time, there are a few things I've learned or ideas that have been reinforced. First of all, BMI is a terrible indicator of health. I could write an entire chapter just on BMI, but I'll leave it at the fact that BMI doesn't take body makeup or muscle mass into consideration at all. There are bodybuilders who are considered obese by BMI standards. Second, the role weight plays in determining our overall health is a lot smaller than we've been led to believe. Last, but certainly not least, being healthy and skinny are not synonymous.

For many, many years, I truly believed that in order to be healthy and fit, you had to look a certain way. That applied to me too, and I believed this as recently as a year ago. After the blood clots, I stopped making goals about losing weight and started making ones about being healthy, but it didn't really matter what I called it because in my mind it meant the same thing: losing enough weight so I *looked* healthy. In my mind, it didn't matter how healthy I actually was if I didn't look the part too. I could talk all day about being healthy and all the healthy habits I have, but no one was ever going to believe me because I was and am still fat. And into today's culture, fat obviously means unhealthy.

That could not be further from the truth. I know there are people out there who will vehemently disagree with me and will say our bodies are not meant to carry so much fat. But what about the fact that our bodies are also not meant to live in starvation mode our entire lives? What about the fact that if we all ate the exact same amount of food and did the exact same workout every single day, we still wouldn't all have the same body type? Just like some people are naturally thin and never have to worry a day in their lives about how much weight eating too much ice cream is going to make them gain, some people are naturally fatter. Just like hair comes in different colors, types, and textures, so do our bodies.

Yes, there are some fat people who are incredibly unhealthy, but there are also some really thin people who are just as unhealthy.

There is no possible way someone can look at a person and know anything about their health. While we are talking about health, I'd like to call bullshit on most of the "concern" there is for fat people's health. Most people aren't concerned about their health, they are just trying to force them into the toxic ideals of what society thinks bodies and health should look like. In most cases, especially ones of bullying on the Internet, concerns for people's health is really just thinly veiled fatphobia.

It doesn't matter what new diet or exercise trend someone recommends because I've tried ALL the diets. I've tried all the quick fixes and the longer-term lifestyle changes, which are really just diets in disguise, and here I am, still fat. Do you know who's not concerned about my fat? My doctor. I firmly believe I shouldn't have to justify my body shape by telling anyone my health stats (because I can guarantee no one is worried about the skinny girl's cholesterol), but since this whole book is about being open and honest, I will.

My work has a health and wellness program that incentivizes employees for being well. Unlike my past job that based the incentive on BMI, my current job bases our incentive on several other health metrics including cholesterol, glucose levels, blood pressure, etc. I've had those tests performed for five years in a row now, and with the exception of when I was eight months pregnant (a quick Google search informed me higher cholesterol is normal in the later stages of pregnancy), my numbers are always within the healthy range. I don't have high blood pressure or high cholesterol, and I'm not anywhere near having prediabetes. I know plenty of skinny people who can't say the same thing. I also don't believe those numbers tell the whole story. I actually believe health and wellness don't have to be tied to weight loss and body size at all.

Health and wellness encompasses so much more than blood pressure, cholesterol, and weight and waist size. Just because I'm eating healthy and working out doesn't mean I am trying to lose weight or change my body. Not all fat people want to be skinny, but that doesn't mean we don't want to be healthy. I try to eat healthy because it gives me energy. I work out because it makes me feel good. Weight loss doesn't always have to be the goal.

Can I walk up a flight of stairs without getting winded? Can I run around the backyard with my toddler without getting tired in five minutes? Do I know which foods make my body feel the best and choose to eat them most of the time? When it comes to some of those things, I still have a lot of work to do. Maybe I'll lose weight as I work toward those goals, maybe I won't, but it doesn't really matter because body size isn't a good indicator of health. Health looks different on everyone and just because I'm fat doesn't mean I'm unhealthy.

CONFESSION 14

I DON'T WANT TO LISTEN TO YOU COMPLAIN ABOUT BEING FAT

I swear to God, if one more person who wears single-digit sized clothing tells me they are fat, I will literally strangle someone. If you can wear a skirt that would fit on one of my thighs, you are not fat. If you have a mostly flat stomach, you are not fat. If you don't have to shop at specialty stores to find your size, you're not fat. If you are not fatter than me, I don't want to listen to you complain about how fat you are.

Until you know what it's like to repeatedly rub holes in the thighs of your pants, to get chafing in between or underneath fat rolls, to not be able to ride certain rides at an amusement park, to need a seat belt extender on an airplane or not fit in most patio chairs, I just don't want to hear it.

You are not fat just because you ate a cookie. You are not fat just because you gained five pounds. You are not fat just because maybe it's that time of the month and your pants are a little tight. You are not fat just because you aren't a size zero. I don't want to have to reassure you over and over again that you are not fat, when really I just want to cry because if you think you're fat, then I must be disgusting.

There have been times when I listened to a friend or family member ramble on and on about how fat they are (despite my best reassurances that they are not) and then gone somewhere by myself and cried because I would kill to be their version of "fat." There have been times when listening to people much skinnier than me whine about being fat that I have wanted to lift up my shirt and say, "You are not fat. This is fat."

I hate that the word fat is used to sum up all the problems we have with our bodies and our confidence. I hate that unless you have the body of a Victoria's Secret model, you've likely been called fat by a bully at some point in your life. I hate it when you commandeer a word that actually describes my body to describe your negative feelings about yourself, i.e., "I feel so fat today." Fat isn't a feeling. It's an actual adjective used to describe how my body looks.

I know, I know, body image issues and self-esteem struggles aren't reserved solely for fat people. I know people of all sizes suffer from body dysmorphia and/or eating disorders. Bodies of all sizes are subjected to the constant bombardment of diet culture and perfectly photoshopped images that make us feel like we are never quite enough. I imagine people of all sizes get upset when they gain weight or when their pants are a little tight after a few days of eating too much. People of all sizes measure their worth based on what the scale says and what size jeans they wear. I KNOW all of those things. I've even had super thin, fit people talk to me about the struggles they have with self-love, but I still can't help but think those people shouldn't be mad about their body because they aren't as fat as me.

How can you call your body fat and complain about it when you wear single-digit sized jeans? Or when you have a flat stomach and thigh gap? How can you complain when you can walk into any store in the mall and find clothing options that fit and flatter your body? How can you complain when you have no cellulite, no fat rolls, and no stretch marks? I know that makes me sound crazy.

I get it. I don't get to hoard all the body hatred and negative body image just because I'm fat. The real problem here isn't my insecurities wanting to have a pity party all to themselves, although that is certainly part of it. The real problem is we have learned through generations of conditioning what is beautiful and acceptable and what is fat and undesirable. We all know this, yet we continue to perpetuate the ideal body type and shape by continually praising those who do manage to reach that ideal.

I think one of my biggest pet peeves is when the people who have actually managed to reach, or at least get close to that ideal body image won't take a compliment; really any compliment, but the ones about body image make me cringe extra hard. How do you think it makes me feel when you are several sizes smaller than me, I tell you you look amazing, and you brush it off with an, "Oh, I've got a long way to go"? Just take the damn compliment!

I don't know what it is about compliments and body size, but for some reason, it seems whenever I complimented someone on how awesome they looked, it always got downplayed. I had one friend in particular who was THE WORST at this. She is one of those people who has had a million kids and still looks better than she did in high school, but no matter how many times I complimented her, I always got some form of the same answer. "Oh, I'm huge," or "I'm still working on it," or "I wish". First of all, when you are half my size and I give you a compliment but you won't accept it, it makes me feel like crap. Second of all, how hard is it to just say thank you?

It is ingrained in our society. If someone posts a transformation photo, they get dozens of likes and compliments proclaiming how good they look. I experienced this firsthand when I used to share transformation photos. They were some of the most liked photos I had, and if I'm being honest, that was the only reason I even posted them. I wanted that validation. I wanted people to know I was getting closer to the skinny body I should have and to praise me for it. I wanted someone to acknowledge all the hard work I'd put in and all the ice cream I didn't eat to get there.

I am as guilty as anybody here. I've shelled out hundreds of compliments based solely on body size and weight over my lifetime. I've told dozens of people how good they look, how skinny they are, and how awesome their body is when they've lost weight.

What message does that send when we only compliment people if they've lost weight? What is that telling little girls about how their bodies should look and little boys about what kind of bodies they should prefer? What message does it send when we all walk around complaining about how fat we are?

While it may seem innocent enough to compliment people on being skinny or talk about your own body behind closed doors, it's not because the next generation is listening. I know because I've heard them call me fat. The first time was when my oldest niece was three. We were out shopping, and I was looking for something to wear to one of my little sister's weddings. I took her hand and led her to the section of the store that carried my size, and she asked me where we were going. I told her to find something that would fit me, and she said, "Yeah, because you're really fat!"

The second time happened just a few months ago at my son's preschool. I was volunteering for the day and was kneeling at the end of the table my son was working at when the little girl sitting closest to me stuck her foot out and poked my stomach with it. She said, "Your belly is really fat." She then proceeded to tell me how her mommy's stomach wasn't fat. In both situations, I didn't know what to say. Maybe they had both just learned about size and shape, and somewhere along the way the word fat was used. It seems more likely, though, that they both heard the word fat being used by people they know, either complaining about their own bodies or making comments about someone else's, and picked it up.

Those seemingly innocent compliments and complaints are keeping us firmly rooted in an era where skinny bodies are preferred over fat ones, and anyone who can't live up is outcast, bullied, or made to feel less than. And in our own eyes, we never meet that standard. Whether you are actually fat or not, when we live in a world that only dishes out compliments when you've lost a noticeable amount of weight, no one is good enough.

I've made it a personal goal of mine to not compliment people on their bodies (or at the very least, not just when their body has gotten smaller), and I'll tell you it is a hard thing to unlearn. There have been multiple times where the words, "You look so good," have bubbled up to the surface, and I've had to bite them back. Not because that person didn't look good but because they are so much more than just a body to be admired and praised. As much as I loved getting compliments like that in the past, they aren't doing anybody any good.

I saw a post on Instagram recently that said, "Stop glorifying weight loss like it's the most impressive thing a human can do." Weight loss is most definitely not the most amazing thing a human can do, but that is the message we send when we hand out compliments to those with fit, thin bodies (and those making their way to that type of body) and hold compliments hostage for people in fatter bodies. We are perpetuating the lie that there is only one "good" body type and that is the body type we should all be striving for. We are setting up another generation for struggling with body image, confidence, self-esteem issues, eating disorders, mental illness, and even self-harm because we are teaching them they aren't worthy of love and acceptance if they don't fit the mold.

I don't want to listen to you complain about being fat, but it's no longer because your words make me feel bad about myself. I don't want to listen to you complain about being fat because there is actually nothing wrong with being fat. Fat isn't a bad thing, and we have to stop giving life to the lie that one size fits all and anyone who doesn't meet the standard is fat.

I don't want to listen to you complain about being fat because if I can hear you, so can little girls and boys who are learning biases from us. If I can hear you, so can someone else who hasn't learned to untangle the web of shame and disgust surrounding their body, and now they are going to purge or cry or beat themselves up because they are fatter than you. I don't want to listen to you complain about being fat because that means we still haven't moved past the preference for skinny bodies, we still haven't figured out how to love and truly accept all bodies, and perhaps most importantly, we haven't figured out how to love ourselves.

CONFESSION 15

I HAVE A LOVE/HATE RELATIONSHIP WITH THE GYM

Oh, the gym. Do any fat girls actually enjoy going to the gym? The gym and I have had a complicated love/hate relationship for the past 15 years. I actually love lifting weights and working out and getting my sweat on, but if someone so much as looks at me wrong, I get super insecure. Am I too fat to be wearing these pants? Do they think I'm kidding myself and should just give up? Are they judging me because I can only do 10 minutes on the treadmill? Are my fat rolls too prominent in this shirt?

I think my issues with the gym and working out, in general, started way back in seventh grade when we all had to participate in the Presidential Fitness tests in front of each other. According to Google, I'm not the only person who was mortified by those fitness tests. Google also reminded me (I've blocked it from my memory) of the five tests: sit-ups, pull-ups, a timed shuttle run, a mile run, and the sit-and-reach, although I swear we did a standing long jump and push-ups too. I failed miserably at everything but the sit-

and-reach. I've always had pretty flexible hamstrings, so I measured off the box in that one, but everything else was not even close. I have never in my entire life been able to do a pull-up, I was too afraid I was going to fart on the person holding my feet to be able to do very many sit-ups (oh, and my abs were weak), and I sucked at running; it didn't matter if it was sprints or long-distance.

I do remember that from seventh grade to the time I was in ninth grade, I improved my mile run time enough to qualify for the lowest level of the award. This was an accomplishment my junior gym teacher shared with anyone who would listen as a lesson in determination.

I don't know if there was anything more embarrassing to 13-year-old me than hanging red-faced from the pull-up bar and not being able to move my body even an inch. Meanwhile, the much skinnier girls in my class could do upwards of 10 pull-ups. It basically scarred me for life and set me up for a lifetime of insecurity in the gym.

Despite my shortcomings in junior high P.E. class, I was an athlete in high school. I played sports year-around and spent hours a week in the gym or weight room when school was in session. I loved playing volleyball, basketball, and softball. Even though I spent a lot of time in the gym and took weightlifting every year of high school, I wasn't very strong. You would think someone my size should be able to bench press more than someone who was 5-foot-4 and 120 pounds, but that wasn't the case. Girls half my size could lift weights far heavier than I could, and that was embarrassing.

I have never been very strong or very fast or very flexible. I've always been sweaty and smelly and awkward. I almost tripped off a treadmill in college because I was too busy watching the NCAA basketball tournament on TV to pay attention to running. I dropped a 45-pound weight plate on myself in high school, and by some miracle I didn't break my foot. I don't always know how different equipment works, and I almost ate it the first time I tried to use a stair-stepper. No matter what kind of workout I'm doing, my fat jiggles or squishes in weird ways, and more than once I've sent my iPod flying across the gym when my headphone cord accidentally gets caught by my swinging hand while running on the treadmill.

What I'm trying to say here is that I'm not a graceful person at the gym, and although I know there are other people like me out there, I seem to always go at the same time as the bikini competitors and stair-stepping queens and guys who look like they drink egg yolks for breakfast. And because every major gym in America has hundreds of mirrors in them so you can watch your form or take dozens of gym selfies, it's a lot easier to notice if anyone is looking at you. It's not like anyone has ever approached me at the gym to voice their disgust, and I've never had one of those experiences where mean-spirited people openly laugh at fat people trying to work out. However, I've still seen people looking at me or have accidentally caught their eye in the mirror, and it immediately sends me into a spiral of self-consciousness.

Am I doing this exercise wrong? Are they thinking I should be able to lift heavier weights? Do they think I'm kidding myself with my BCAAs in my water bottle? Are my big rose gold Beats headphones out of place? Is there a better order to be doing my exercises in? Is my fat jiggling too much? Basically, any ridiculous thought you could think someone else might be having about you at the gym has crossed my mind.

I'm super competitive by nature (thanks, Dad), so I want to be good at whatever I do. It's not enough to just do something I want to excel at it. I want to be able to lift heavy weights, be flexible, and run fast, and it doesn't matter if it's physically impossible, I want to be able to do a headstand in yoga, damn it!

This is the very vain part of me speaking, but I want to look good doing these things. I don't mean good like the girls who somehow never sweat and still have perfect makeup and hair after the gym, but good as in that girl actually looks like she belongs here and knows what she's doing. Basically, not like the imposter I've felt like my entire life. When I was in college and would go work out at the field house, I would avoid the free weights like the plague because there was always a group of guys who looked like football players hanging around them. It didn't matter that using free weights is probably what I am best at, I wasn't about to walk my fat ass past several attractive guys to grab the 10-pound dumbbells and do a few bicep curls.

The college field house is probably a terrible example because if there is anywhere that people are paying more attention to those around them than their own workout, that is probably it. But I think in most cases, people are too busy getting through their own workouts or having their own inner monologue about the guy who just looked at them wrong to even notice what I am doing, let alone if I'm doing it wrong.

Not only realizing, but making my crazy brain believe, that other people probably don't even notice—much less judge—me has been a huge help in overcoming my self-esteem issues at the gym. More often than not, people are too caught up in themselves or you know, actually working out, to be worrying about what random strangers at the gym are doing. More often than not, all of that judgment is just in my head.

But even if they are judging me, why should I let the opinions of people I don't even know keep me from doing the workouts I love? Why should I let the fear of being noticed at the gym keep me from going in the first place? Why should I worry about what other people are thinking if I go to the gym every day for six months and don't lose any weight?

The gym is time for me. I have to assume that unless you are a bodybuilder or fitness model by profession, you are at the gym because you want to be, or at the very least have a really motivating reason for being there. What other people think (or more likely what I think other people think) shouldn't stop me from enjoying the time I have to work out and focus on improving myself.

For now, I do most of my workouts at home because two small children and a husband with a schedule opposite of mine makes anything else mostly impossible, but one day I'll go back to the gym. One day, I'll walk back into a gym with my Beats headphones and a water bottle full of fruity BCAAs and not give a damn about what anyone else thinks. One of the most beautiful parts of finding self-love and body positivity is the ability to let go of all the insecurities and made-up expectations I have been carrying around for years, and instead, just do my own thing without a second thought.

CONFESSION 16

I PRETEND TO BE CONFIDENT AND HAPPY BUT I'M NOT

"You call yourself Fat Amy?"

"Yeah, so twig bitches like you don't do it behind my back."

I don't know if there has ever been a line from a movie that resonated with me so much. If you haven't seen *Pitch Perfect*, you should go watch it immediately because it's hilarious, and Fat Amy is my spirit animal. While I don't go so far as to call myself "Fat Paige" like Amy does, I know exactly what she's talking about because if I've ever made a joke about myself, it's so you can't do it first. If I've ever been the loud, outspoken one, it's so maybe you would just think I was funny instead of fat. If I've ever seemed confident and sure of myself, it was probably all an act, one I've been perfecting since I was a child.

I learned at a young age that people were going to make fun of me no matter what. Whether it was because I was fat or tall or had a name that was easy to make jokes with, there was always someone ready to make fun of me, so I might as well at least control the things they made fun of me for. It always stings when someone makes fun of you, but it stings less if they do for the reasons you give them instead of the ones they make up on their own. It doesn't hurt quite as bad when you're in on the joke.

That meant in sixth grade I leaned back in my chair, talked to every person I could during class (even the ones who didn't sit by me), and got assigned more initiatives than I could ever count as a result. It meant in junior high I continued talking to anyone and everyone in class, cracking jokes about everything from the weather to our teachers. If I was going to get made fun of, it was going to be because I got separated from the rest of the math class in eighth grade, not because I was bigger than everyone else. It meant in high school I told my close friends I was dating boys I wasn't (I don't have to tell you how well that went over in a small high school) and let the older boys I had crushes on cheat off me in math class so I could seem like I was cool. It meant in college I was always the fun, drunk friend who accidentally broke things when I'd had too many drinks.

My false confidence led me to try out for the women's basketball team when I was a freshman in college, even though I had no business being there. It convinced me to try out for *American Idol*, even though I'm not a great singer. It made me brave enough to help spell penis in the drop caps of our senior goodbye columns at my college newspaper.

I didn't feel confident or truly happy in any of those instances or dozens of others where it seemed like I did, but it was easier to hide behind fake confidence than let people see my real thoughts and show my real emotions.

There are literally hundreds of times when I might have been smiling and looking like I was having a good time, but I was almost always thinking what it would be like to be one of the skinny friends who actually got dates or hit on by boys. I was thinking about how much I hated my body and wished I were shorter and smaller. I was thinking about how fat and disgusting all these people must think I am. But I never actually said that out loud because no one wants to hang out with a Debbie Downer. No one wants to be friends with the fat, sad girl. So instead I told stories and jokes, I always had something to say, and I always brought the story or conversation back around to me so I could make sure people knew how funny and witty I was, even if I really wasn't.

I always went with the flow. I rarely had opinions about what we should do or where we should go on any given night because I didn't dare be bigger and more outspoken than everyone else. I always felt like I needed to be the fun, easygoing friend.

I sometimes wonder if I am actually as sarcastic as I am naturally or if I used it as a defense mechanism for so long that now it's just a part of who I am. I developed faux confidence, an aloof attitude, and a lot of sarcasm, but at night I would cry myself to sleep and wish I could be just like everyone else and didn't have to pretend all the damn time.

I have acted like I didn't give a shit what people thought for years when in reality I cared entirely too much. I cared about everything they thought about me from my weight, to my clothes, to my hair, to my terrible dance moves. I can't count how many times I've pretended to be having a good time when I wanted nothing more than to curl up in a ball and cry. There have been times when I couldn't fight it anymore, when I would get totally lost in my own thoughts and space everyone else out until someone called my name and brought me back to being happy and confident.

Living that life is exhausting. Going about your day-to-day interactions pretending and hiding your true feelings—hiding your true self—is one of the worst ways to live. Having to constantly put on a front is tiring and no fun, but it is easier than being vulnerable. It is easier and less scary than letting people see the real you. My closest friends are going to read this book and learn more things than they ever probably wished to know about me because there are some parts of me I've kept hidden from everyone.

The dark, insecure parts. The parts that spend too much time thinking about weight and size and being skinny. The parts that keep me awake at night wondering how much plastic surgery would cost to get rid of all my fat and extra skin. The parts that wish I could be as skinny as those friends. The parts that are sure everyone is judging me for having a second cookie. The parts I wish I could cut out and throw in the garbage.

I, however, have learned in the past year and from the incredible Brene Brown that being vulnerable and authentic is the only way to truly live. If you haven't heard of or read anything from Brene Brown you should do it as soon as you finish this book. She is a shame researcher turned author who has fascinating and amazing things to say about shame, fitting in, and being vulnerable, and her books have literally changed my life.

Letting down my guard and finally showing some of my true emotions is so freeing. It honestly feels like a weight has been lifted off my shoulders. It is liberating to show my emotions and let people know I don't have all my shit together. It feels good to share that I cried when I was getting dressed this morning because nothing fits and have so many people respond with their own versions of the same story. It is so freeing to finally stop pretending.

I wish I could say that means I've stopped caring what people think altogether, but there are still plenty of times I care too much. There are still many times I revert back to my old, comfortable ways because I'm still a work in progress, and changing the habits you've had for most of your life is really hard. I've realized I don't have to pretend to be confident 24/7 because no one else is either. I don't have to act like everything is okay because sometimes it's just not. I don't always have to be the loud, attention-seeking friend just so people don't notice my body.

I've noticed as I've become more confident—real confidence, not the fake shit I've been projecting my whole life—I've become quieter. I listen a lot more than I used to. I don't always feel the need to interject my story or opinion into every single conversation. I don't need to bring all the attention to me because I finally know what I bring to the table. I finally know I am more than just the funny fat girl.

CONFESSION 17

I GAVE AWAY MY BODY IN ORDER TO FEEL LOVED

Mom, you should probably just skip this chapter because what I'm about to say here is guaranteed to make you wonder if I learned any of the lessons you tried to teach me growing up. You know, the ones about remembering who you are and where you came from and what you stand for. That all sounds nice and easy until you are a 20-year-old who's never been kissed.

I've read or heard stories of girls as young as 12 or 13 having sex with much older boys because the boys were popular, and the girls had lacked any real love in their lives up until that point and were craving any type of affection. This isn't one of those stories. Well, maybe the affection part. To say I was inexperienced as a teenager would be an understatement. I got asked on one date the entire time I was in high school, and it was to prom. I was asked by a guy my friends set me up with, so I'm not even sure that counts.

I vividly remember being at a volleyball team bonfire my junior year in high school when we all went around sharing our dirtiest secret about boys (or something like that, I honestly don't remember what we were even talking about), and my big confession at the time was a dream I had about the boy I had a crush on at the time. No make out sessions in the back of the car or inappropriate touching, just a dream that I'm almost positive I made up just to get a reaction from my teammates.

College did not change anything. My freshman year of college I was awkward, self-conscious, and basically terrified of boys. On top of that, I never really went anywhere but my dorm room or class or the dining hall, so the boys I met and hung out with were limited to the guys my roommates dated.

My twentieth birthday came and went with me never having held anyone's hand, never having been kissed, never having been asked on a date, and never getting any sort of attention from guys. It was more than a little depressing.

Everything changed in just one night. It was a Saturday in January, and I was at work texting my friend about how I was going to die having never been kissed because I was overly dramatic like that. Later that night, we went to a party at the home of several wildland firefighters, one of whom my friend was dating. We had been there before, hung out, and played beer pong with most of the people there. There was a lot of drinking, like there always was, and I don't even know what time it was when I finally lay down on the couch and willed the room to stop spinning so I could go to sleep. Then the least attractive of the firefighters asked me to come to his bedroom.

I actually wrote three whole pages about what happened next because in case you haven't noticed, writing is how I process my feelings, but I'll spare you all the gory details and just skip to the important part. I went from never being kissed to third base in the span of 45 minutes with a guy whose name and occupation were the only things I knew about him. I'm honestly not even sure if he knew my name, but in that drunken moment, it didn't matter. It didn't matter that he had a different girl in his room earlier that night or that I was supposed to be going to my Mormon sorority meeting the next morning. All that mattered was for the first time ever, someone was paying attention to me.

What happened in that bedroom went against everything I had been taught growing up, and I went through a mini life crisis after it happened that included cutting my hair in the most unflattering haircut of all time. But that night, when my friends were with their boyfriends and I was all alone, the idea that maybe someone did want me or I wasn't repulsive made me feel desirable for the first time in my life. It wouldn't be the last time I'd visit that particular firefighter's bedroom without us ever learning any more about each other. It also wouldn't be the last time I'd take my clothes off for a guy I barely knew.

I remember when I was in high school, there were certain girls who always had boyfriends. Not the pretty, popular girls, but the ones who smoked cigarettes behind the bleachers. I used to wonder how *those* girls always had boyfriends, but I couldn't even get a date to the prom. How did girls who didn't look like they showered regularly and who I thought I was prettier than always have someone hanging on them? I finally understood. They put out.

I am fairly confident in saying now that Mr. Firefighter didn't really think I was super attractive or desirable, but rather I was the only option available in those few instances, and I was willing. Still to this day, when I think about that night or that firefighter I gave a handful of my firsts to, I cringe. Partly because I wasn't attracted to him, but more because of how little I valued myself. I gave him those pieces of myself because I truly believed no one else would ever want them, that I didn't deserve anything or anyone better. I have no doubt if it hadn't been him, it would've been someone else in similar circumstances because at that time in my life, I wanted more than anything to be loved. To be accepted. To be wanted. And I equated the sexual desires of drunk 20-somethings with those feelings.

I wanted nothing more than to know I wasn't completely hopeless and that my body wasn't disgusting and unlovable. Up until that point, my lack of physical (or any) relationship with boys was a clear indicator to me that I wasn't accepted or desirable or that I didn't have any of the things men wanted in a partner. But it's hard to feel undesirable when your body is getting showered with attention. In those moments, it was easy to forget about how fat and unattractive I thought I was and focus on how good it felt for someone to finally pay attention to me.

The high that came from finally feeling "loved" was always short-lived. I was hurt the next time I saw Mr. Firefighter and he acted like he had no idea who I was. After he initiated things a few times, I got brave and tried to do the same, only to get rejected. I was crushed. I was back to feeling like I had before, except worse. When the only thing a person knows about you is how you look naked, it's only logical to assume they turned you down because they found someone better, or worse, they never really thought you were attractive in the first place. Rather, they were just looking for anyone willing to help satisfy their urges, and that hurts.

That hurt, however, didn't stop me from getting myself into the same situation several more times. It didn't stop me from seeking validation and "love" in the only way I knew how. It didn't stop me from continuing to give guys parts of me they didn't deserve in an effort to feed my desperate hunger to be loved. The high of finally being accepted and "loved" was worth the pain and hurt that would eventually follow.

It sounds crazy now, but when you've spent your whole life looking for validation, *finally* being noticed feels so good. When you have no self-esteem or confidence of your own, you believe you aren't worth anything more and you'll take what you can get.

I think there are only two ways out of this cycle. One: realize you deserve better and believe you are worth more than being some drunk boy's booty call. Or two: find someone who treats you better and breaks the cycle. I firmly believe my cycle would've continued for much longer than it did if I hadn't met my husband.

Our relationship started out much the same: solely physical but minus the drunken 2:00 a.m. escapades. We actually went out together in the light of day, and he texted me back, and I didn't have to sneak out of his room the next morning hoping no one would catch me doing the walk of shame. In addition to finding someone who broke my cycle of booty calls/hating myself, I also began to realize love encompassed so much more than just the physical. I realized guys (or at least this guy) liked things about me that had nothing to do with my body.

His love didn't immediately cure me and all my body woes, but it did make me realize I deserved more than the fake love and attention-for-all-the-wrong-reasons I had been getting. Because no matter what the reason is for turning to physical intimacy for validation, that kind of attention never truly fills the void. It never truly makes you feel loved, and it never truly makes you feel any better about yourself. Whether you give yourself to one person or a hundred, none of it feels good in the long run because eventually the sun comes up and everything looks different in the light of day.

I think back on that time in my life and feel sad for the girl who thought she was so worthless. I feel sad for all the girls and women around the world who feel that exact same way right now and are putting their worth in the hands of people who don't deserve it and are looking for love in all the wrong places. I want to tell them they are worth so much more than that. That even though they can't imagine it, there are people out there who will love them for everything they are in the light of day, and even if they never find that person, they are still loved and worthy of love. I want to tell them they are worth more than being someone's booty call when they think that's all they deserve. I want to tell them the love they are looking for can't be found with strangers who don't even know their name.

But if someone had told me that 15 years ago, I wouldn't have listened anyway because sometimes you have to walk through the darkness to find the light.

CONFESSION 18

I REFUSE TO DANCE OR WORK OUT IN FRONT OF YOU

If there is even a remote possibility that any of my body parts will jiggle or I might get sweaty or out of breath, I don't want to do it, at least not anywhere that people who know me can see. If there is any way someone might see me and think, "She is way too big to be doing that," I'm out. Yoga, dancing, strenuous hiking, it's all out. Unless you give me several shots of tequila, then I'll gladly dance the night away with you.

I can't pinpoint exactly when this refusal started because I played sports in high school. I ran up and down the basketball court, jumped and jiggled playing volleyball, and wore bright blue pants that were probably a size too small playing softball. But back then, in my tiny town, I knew I had at least some skill, and that gave me a little bit of confidence. It didn't really matter if my butt looked huge in my white basketball shorts because I was fairly good at basketball. It didn't matter if my volleyball shorts showed too much of my thighs because I just loved volleyball and was decent at that too. I got sweaty and smelly and my fat wiggled all over the place, but I didn't mind because there was always someone ready to tell me "good job" after each game.

Out in the big world, where there is always someone better than you, confidence in your abilities and your body is hard to come by. I'm unwilling to put myself in a situation where anyone can see I have no skill or can judge my body. It's not even just dancing or working out. I'd really rather not go on hikes or walks up big hills or flights of stairs with you either. Do you know how hard it is to try and breathe normally when you're really out of breath? Do you know how hard it is to act like you're not going to die and have a conversation with your not-out-of-breath skinny friends? And if I'm breathing super hard, then of course you are going to think that all I do at night is sit on the couch and eat ice cream instead of doing a workout like I should.

I tried to get over this when I was in college. I went to a Zumba class with a couple of friends. A couple of friends who had been on the drill team in high school and actually had rhythm. I stood in the back of the class and half-danced, half-flapped my arms around like an idiot for the hour-long class. I watched my friends (and dozens of other women) bust out moves I would never be able to do. I was uncomfortable the entire time, and I never went back. Okay, so maybe I didn't try very hard to get over it.

It hasn't just been workout classes either. I still, to this very day, feel uncomfortable dancing with friends (again, unless I'm very, very drunk). Being fat my whole life has messed up my knees, and I can't dance like I think a 30-year-old should be able to dance. I am completely aware of how ridiculous this all sounds, but when you've been the fat, out-of-shape friend your entire life, you don't need more situations that remind you one of these things is not like the other. You don't need to intentionally put yourself in situations that make you feel uncomfortable about your body because those opportunities come often enough all by themselves.

But you see, while I was refusing to participate in all these activities with my friends, the only person putting me down was myself. The only person missing out on the fun was me. Aside from a few mean comments from dumb boys in high school, no one has ever made fun of me or said anything about my body during workouts, hikes, walking around cities, etc. Not even once. I projected my own inner insecurities onto them. If someone gave me a "weird" glance at the gym, I would automatically assume they were thinking I didn't belong there. I know there are a lot of cruel people out there. There are people who do make fun of fat people at the gym or yell rude comments at the ones brave enough to go running outside, but I have never in my life encountered one. Maybe it's because I have resting bitch face and people don't want to piss me off, or maybe it's because whenever I work out, I listen to ridiculously loud music and wouldn't be able to hear derogatory comments even if people were making them. Or maybe, and most likely, it's because no one gives a shit, and all the negativity is just in my head.

As much as I'd like to pretend I'm a badass that scares people off, I know the correct answer is the last one. All the negativity is just in my head. All the things I've held myself back from doing over the years are because of me and my unwillingness to be uncomfortable. Sure, I didn't really want other people to see how out of shape and uncoordinated I was, but more than that, I was hiding from myself. I hated my body. I hated all the things it couldn't do, from doing Zumba to not being able to do a push-up. I refused to put myself in situations where I would be reminded of all the things I wasn't capable of. I blamed it on not wanting to be made fun of, but really I wasn't able to step outside of my comfort zone. I wasn't willing to push my body and learn new things because I was certain it would just be one more thing my body would fail at.

It would be more than a decade after my Zumba experience before I went to another group fitness class. A time in which I experienced exponential amounts of growth in terms of maturity and confidence. A time in which I learned to care a lot less about what other people think of my body and embrace the things that make me feel good.

When I did return to a group workout class, it was to a yoga session with one of my good friends. I had been practicing yoga in the safety of my living room for a few months and was excited but nervous to finally try an in-person class. When I got there, all those feelings of insecurity and discomfort came rushing back. I felt embarrassment about my extra-large yoga mat and uncertainty about my abilities. I don't look like most of the people I've seen that are passionate about yoga or most of the people in my class.

I love yoga because the focus is very much on you and where you are today. In both the online and in-person classes I've attended, the instructors were very open and welcoming. They encouraged us to make modifications as we need them and not worry about forcing our body into the yoga shapes we'd seen before. Rather, the focus was on experiencing the movements and sensations. Even with the instruction to focus on myself and my own experience, I found my mind wandering. Full confession: I'm still really terrible at the meditation and mindset part of yoga. My mind always wanders, usually to all the things I have to do later, but this time it wandered back into old familiar territory.

I couldn't help but wonder if I was doing it right or if anyone noticed when I had to take a knee or use a modification or that I'm not very flexible. I couldn't help but wonder if anyone noticed that mine was the biggest body in the room and that I definitely didn't look like I belonged. I was more than halfway through the class before I stopped myself from that all too familiar dialogue in my head. Despite the fact that no one was looking at me and was engrossed in their own practice and thoughts, it was still so easy to let my mind take me back to the time when I thought everyone was watching and wondering why I thought I belonged here.

When I finally stopped thinking about and wondering what other people were thinking, I enjoyed myself. It honestly didn't matter that I couldn't do every pose or flow perfectly, I was there doing yoga and loving it. My body may not be perfect, but in those moments it was strong, it was resilient, and it wasn't failing me. I had pushed myself out of my comfort zone and had an amazing experience I would've otherwise missed out on. It makes me wonder how many things I've missed out on over the years. How many more amazing experiences could I have had? How many other experiences did I talk myself out of because I was afraid of pushing my body or afraid that someone might see me fail?

My body isn't perfect. It isn't the skinniest or the best at dancing or running or yoga. It isn't fast and can't jump very high, and it will probably never be able to fulfill my weird obsession with being able to do the splits. But there are a lot of amazing things it can do, and those things deserve to be celebrated. There are a lot more experiences waiting for me out there, and if I can get out of my own way, my body is going to allow me to do them. Regardless of the negativity I've spent years projecting on other people, no one really gives a damn about what my body looks like when I work out or dance. And if they do, I'll be too busy jamming out to my music and enjoying myself to care.

CONFESSION 19

I EAT IN SECRET SO NO ONE CAN SHAME ME

If a tree falls in the forest and no one is there to hear it, does it still make a sound? If I eat an entire carton of ice cream but no one sees, did it really happen?

I eat in secret. A lot. Sometimes even when I'm really hungry, I'll eat in private because as a fat person, I'm supposed to be eating less. I'm supposed to be watching what I eat and making healthy changes. I'm not supposed to eat ice cream or cookies or tacos. So I eat where no one can see me because if no one knows what or when or how much I'm eating, then no one can have anything to say about it.

It probably goes without saying, but I'm self-conscious about what I eat in front of you. It doesn't matter if you are my mom or a stranger at Starbucks, eating in front of people makes me uncomfortable. Are my skinny friends judging me when I get a second helping of guac? What about when I order dessert? Are you thinking to yourself that this is why I'm fat? If I eat too much cheese or too many chips with salsa, are you all judging me?

I can tell you the exact moment this started for me. I remember it all very clearly; from the chair I was sitting in, to the bowl I was eating out of. It was Christmastime. You know, the time when there are so many sweets and treats it's a miracle that everyone doesn't go into a sugar coma. I was 12 or 13, maybe a little older, and I had spent several days eating treats and all the other yummy Christmas food just like everyone else in the family. I was sitting in the living room in our big brown recliner by the window as it snowed outside. I was eating broccoli, cauliflower, and carrots out of a bowl of vegetables with ranch dip when a family member stormed in, ripped the bowl out of my hands, and yelled at me to stop eating. I remember the tears welling up in my eyes as I argued that they were just vegetables. It didn't matter. They said I didn't need to eat any more; enough was enough.

I have to hold back the tears as I write this because that moment is still painful for me to remember. I was shamed and yelled at for eating vegetables, and I still remember how startling it was to have that bowl ripped out of my hands. Had I eaten a ton of sweets and treats and rolls and everything else? I have no doubt that I had, but so had all the other kids. So had my sisters and my cousins, but I was the only one getting yelled at for eating vegetables. That person was right. I probably didn't need to eat any more. I probably did need to stop eating, even if they were vegetables, but how much I was eating isn't important. What's important is that I learned to eat where no one could see me.

I took that experience, and I internalized it. Hard. I would sneak any sweets or "forbidden" foods I was eating. I would eat any snacks I had when no one was around or wait until they all went to bed. I still do this, to this very day. I stand in the kitchen at work and eat a leftover piece of cake instead of taking it back to my desk where people can see me. I eat most of my after-dinner snacks and desserts while my husband is in the shower or before he gets home from work. And if I happen to get caught, the embarrassment I feel is sometimes enough to make me blush.

I wish I only had that one bad experience with being food shamed, but I have plenty more. I've been asked more times than I care to count, "Should you be eating that? Do you really need seconds? Isn't that bad for you? Aren't you on a diet?" And let me tell you, no one asks skinny girls if they should be eating something or if something has too many calories in it. As a fat girl, I've obviously lost all control around food and need random people to police my eating. But if I eat an entire pint of ice cream all alone on my couch, no one says a damn thing. If I go back for seconds later when everyone else is otherwise occupied, no one looks at me with disgust. If I eat in secret, I know no one is judging me but myself.

Not only am I fat, but I also eat really fast. I get that from my mom. Since I was a little girl, she has always been the first person to finish eating at dinner. She's told us more than once it is a result of having three brothers who would literally eat off her plate if she didn't finish before them. With three sisters and plenty of food in our house, I have no such survival instinct to blame for my fast eating, but it's a habit I still picked up from her. I am now routinely one of the first people done eating when I go out with friends or we have potlucks at work. I am constantly trying to force myself to slow down and sometimes even leave food on my plate so people won't judge me for how much or how fast I ate.

There was one time my husband and I went out to dinner. We had ordered appetizers, but they came with our meal. Our waitress disappeared for a solid 20 minutes, and when she returned, we were nearly finished eating. She stood at the end of our table with her hands on her hips and said, "Wow, you guys did work." My face turned red, and I turned away with embarrassment. Note to servers in the world: if you want a good tip or any tip at all, don't comment on how much or how fast your customers are eating.

If I eat by myself, I don't have to worry about any of that. I can eat my food as fast as I want. I can go back for seconds. I can eat dessert before dinner or instead of dinner if I feel like it. I don't have to listen to anyone's opinions or wonder if they have opinions and are just trying to be civilized human beings.

There have been times I have actually pretended I wasn't hungry so I didn't have to eat in front of people. There have been times when I've lied about how hungry I was because I didn't want the people I was with to think, "Damn, is that girl eating *again?*" I'm not talking about stopping myself from snacking when I'm not hungry. I'm talking about ignoring my physical hunger cues and sometimes pushing myself to the point of being physically ill, all because the shame of eating in front of people can be overwhelming strong sometimes. Please, someone tell me I am not alone in this because I'm starting to think I might actually be a crazy person.

Actually, I know I'm not alone because right now the hashtag #womeneatingfood is floating around Instagram. The idea is that women should be able to eat and enjoy food, not just salads, in public and on social media without fear of judgment or criticism. You guys, how insane is it that women need a hashtag to be able to show our face enjoying food? As crazy as it seems, I totally get it because I am one of those people hiding in shame.

I'm trying really hard to let this go because it doesn't matter how fat I am, I still have to eat. My body still needs food to survive, and I shouldn't have to hide in shame anytime I eat. And more than just needing food to survive, just because I'm fat doesn't mean I should have to live a boring life eating salads and green smoothies from now until the end of time. Food and eating is an inherently social thing, and I should get to enjoy food just as much as my skinny friends. I shouldn't have to apologize for wanting dessert every single day. I shouldn't have to order the salad when I really want tacos just because I'm afraid of what people might think. I shouldn't have to say no to Fat Pill Friday (donuts) at work just because I weigh more than some of the other people in my office. I should get to live and enjoy food just as much as everyone else.

I know these things. I know all these things are true, but I still struggle. I still hide. I still feel guilt and shame. I never said I was perfect.

CONFESSION 20

I'M AFRAID OF LOSING ALL THE WEIGHT

As a fat person, my only goal in life is supposed to be to lose all the weight and finally free the skinny girl living inside me. To finally get skinny so I can be happy. But instead of being excited about all the possibilities that could await me if I were no longer fat, the idea of being skinny scares me. Is that really even believable? What kind of person is afraid of losing weight? Stay with me for a minute.

That might sound ridiculous, but I've read a lot of personal development books and blogs over the past year, and I've seen several times that it's often not the fear of failure that holds us back but the fear of success. I've read that we sabotage our own success and happiness because we are actually afraid of how our lives might change if we get there. In order to make myself feel better about being crazy, I tend to think this fear is along those same lines.

If you go by BMI or even what my goal weight would be, I have somewhere between 85-120 pounds to lose at minimum. Losing that much weight would put me at a weight I haven't been my entire adult life, and the idea of losing all the weight I've gained and lost and gained back again terrifies me. I'm afraid I'll lose all my curves. I'm afraid I'll have gross extra skin and my husband won't think I'm attractive anymore. I'm afraid I won't know how to be a skinny person. I'm afraid if I lose too much weight, I'll look like a hypocrite for preaching about body positivity and loving yourself just the way you are (I know that's not the point of body positivity but still, I'm afraid). I'm afraid I'll have to spend the rest of my life dieting and working out constantly to maintain all that weight loss. I'm afraid I won't ever be able to eat my favorite foods again. I'm afraid of all the things I'd have to give up and maybe miss out on while I'm trying to get skinny. I'm afraid once I get there, I won't be me anymore.

I've thought about finally losing all the weight for years and what it would be like to have a semi-flat stomach. I've thought about how it would feel to walk into any store I want and find my size. I've thought about how it would feel to wear a real bikini or a crop top or be able to tuck in a shirt without worrying if it made my fat rolls look bigger. I've thought about all the things that would be better in my life when I'm not fat anymore, but despite all those thoughts, I can't actually picture it. I can picture in detail the house I want to build or what my imaginary book characters look like, but I don't have any idea what a skinny Paige looks like.

I can't imagine how different it would be to get rid of the fat rolls I've had forever. I can't imagine what my face would look like and how clothes would fit. I can't picture how my crazy curly hair would look with a skinny face. It's hard to imagine how my body would move if it had 100 fewer pounds to carry around. For someone who has spent so much time fantasizing about being skinny, you'd think I would be able to at least describe what I'd look like, but I can't. Maybe it's because I have serious doubts that I'll ever get there. Maybe it's because even when I was in high school and as close to my "ideal weight" as I've ever been, I still wasn't skinny. Maybe it's because I'm afraid, and not picturing it is my mind's way of keeping me safe in the land of fat girls.

I have no doubt that my biggest physical fear is extra skin. You've seen those pictures on the Internet of some women holding all her extra skin from her stomach and pulling it away from her body, and then there's another shot of it hanging down in front of her. I'm afraid of becoming that person. And the skin on your stomach you can hide, but what about my arms or my thighs? What about all the parts I can't hide? I know, being healthy should be more important than being vain about extra skin, but I can't help it. I don't really want to look like an 80-year-old with skin hanging off my body when I'm 35. I don't want to have to go back to wearing tops that have sleeves and Bermuda shorts because I'm ashamed of my body for a whole different reason. I spend too much time on Google researching it, so now the idea of skin removal surgery terrifies me. Or even worse, what if I lose all the weight and then somehow found the money to get all my extra skin removed, only to gain all that weight back *again?*

It's not only skin, though. I go through a constant battle of wanting to lose weight and get skinny and not wanting to lose my curves. I like my butt and my boobs, but for some reason, those are always the first places I lose weight! Why can't I lose weight from my belly instead of the places I actually like?! What if I lose all those things and just end up looking like a linebacker because of my big shoulders? I'm kind of fond of my cleavage and the way my butt looks in pencil skirts, and so is my husband. I don't want to lose those things on my way to becoming my skinniest self.

Even more than skin and body parts I actually like, I'm afraid if I was skinny I wouldn't be me anymore. In case you haven't figured it out by now, I have spent my entire life as the fat friend. I have been plus-sized my entire adult life. I have *always* been fat. I have built my entire personality and now an entire brand around being a big girl. What the hell would I do if I were a skinny person?

I'm not naive enough to think I would suddenly have all the confidence I was always missing growing up or that my relationship with food would suddenly become uncomplicated, but I think it would be equally naive to assume I wouldn't change at all either. I think it's kind of like winning the lottery. No matter how much people say they will still be the same, that big of a life change will inevitably have some impact on who you are and how you act.

What if no one liked new, skinny Paige? What if I were annoyingly conceited? Would I still need all the defense mechanisms I developed as a fat person over the years? If I were no longer the fat friend, how would that change the dynamic of my friendships? Would I think I was better than those people now? Would I lose friends because I was no longer the go-to fat friend? How would it change my marriage? How would it change my everyday life?

What if I did all that work and nothing changed? What if I lost all that weight and I was still the fat friend? What if I still struggled with confidence and food freedom and loving my new body? What if I was finally skinny and still hated myself?

Yes, I know my mind is a crazy place to be, but those are big, scary questions to consider. And I'm afraid to find out the answers to some of those questions. I might be the only fat person on the planet who is scared to lose a lot of weight and finally reach the elusive goal of being skinny, but I am. How dumb would it be to finally reach the goal I've been striving for my entire life and have the rest of my life fall apart?

What it boils down to is the fear of the unknown. I don't know how to be a skinny person. Even though I've prayed for it to happen a million times, I don't actually know how being skinny would change my life, and that's scary.

Just like any other fear I've faced in my life, writing this book being one of them, I have to stop and ask myself what I really, truly want out of life and how overcoming my fear is going to help me get there. I have to make a million lists of pros and cons and talk to myself in the car about how bad I want it or not. I have to think about all the time and effort it's going to take to do whatever scary thing I'm trying to talk myself out of and ask, "Is it worth it?" When it comes to pushing past my fears, going all in, and losing 100 pounds, I'm just not sure the answer is yes.

CONFESSION 21

CONFIDENT, OUT-THERE GIRLS WILL ALWAYS AMAZE ME

My husband and I were watching *Chicago Fire* on TV one night when a girl on the show took one of the hot firefighter's phones, put her number in it, and gave it back to him with some not-so-subtle comment about what he should do with it.

The conversation that followed pretty much went like this.

"Do girls really do that?" I asked.

"Some girls do."

"I would literally never do that."

"That's because you don't think you are one of the hot ones."

"I'm not one of the hot ones."

"See, that's your problem."

Bless my cute husband for thinking I'm one of the hot ones. But let's pretend for one second that I too thought I was one of the hot ones. Putting myself out there like that would literally never happen in a million years. I don't think I've ever even initiated a conversation with a guy at a bar, let alone just walked up, given him my phone number, and suggested he call me later for a hookup.

Do girls like that never get rejected? Or do they just not care because if they get rejected by one guy, there is another one waiting to take them home instead? In situations like that, you are really just putting your body on a platter and hoping someone will take it. You aren't trying to find a stable relationship, and that guy certainly doesn't care about your sparkling personality. My non-existent confidence could never do it because when they inevitably do say no, it is nothing but a rejection of my body. It's one more reminder it's not good enough and that I'm not desirable. It's just one more reason why I should stay home and eat Oreos instead of going out and trying to find someone who wants my fat body.

Actually, I lied. I did put myself out there once, and it ended very badly. I was in college and got brave enough one day to text a guy I knew for a booty call (sorry, Mom) instead of the other way around. You know what his answer was? "No, thanks." Like I had offered him a piece of chocolate instead of my body. I was crushed. Like, ridiculously crushed. I started to cry in the back seat of my friend's Jeep and had to hurry inside to hide my tears when we arrived home so my friend and her boyfriend wouldn't see me crying. I probably cried myself to sleep that night like I did so many times in high school because no one asked me out. Ever. It was a new and different kind of rejection, but that didn't make it feel any better.

I invited another friend over a few nights later and got completely wasted in an effort to forget about it. When that didn't work, I got a really bad haircut and enrolled in the counseling services offered by the university I was attending. It took three months of therapy and losing 15 pounds to get even a tiny bit of my already low confidence back.

It didn't take very long in therapy to figure out why I was struggling with the rejection so much. I was crushed because I had offered my body up on a silver platter, and it got pushed aside like Brussels sprouts at Thanksgiving dinner. He wasn't rejecting my personality because, let's be real, we barely knew each other. Maybe he just didn't want to get involved with a young, inexperienced college student. In my mind, all I could think about was how disgusting my body must be that I could offer him everything I had and he just said, "No, thanks." And that hurt. It reinforced the message I had been getting over and over again my entire life, which was that my body wasn't good enough and that it wasn't worth loving. There was/is no way I would ever do that again.

I wish I could say I had an eye-opening experience when I was in therapy, but 20-year-old me was probably the worst therapy patient of all-time. I shared a few things about my past and family life, a few things that were maybe connected to the shame I was feeling, but most of the things we talked about were surface-level because I was too afraid to dig deep and look at the real issues. I was too afraid to open up and really talk about what I was feeling and why. And as soon as I started to lose a little weight and felt a tiny bit better about myself, I bolted because running from my feelings was a lot easier than facing them at the time.

Now I can clearly see why I was so hurt by those two little words. I was looking for outside sources of validation. I was relying on other people to give me my confidence, and in turn, I gave them the power to take it away in an instant. I let myself believe that because one guy had turned me down, it meant I was unlovable. It meant no one would ever want me or my body, and I was going to die alone. I wanted just one person to like my body, so maybe then I could give myself permission to like it too. I was looking for someone to want me so I would finally have a reason to be confident.

But that's not how confidence works, or at least that's not how healthy confidence works. That will forever be the difference between those girls like the one on TV and me. They are confident in themselves. Maybe their confidence comes from never getting rejected or knowing there will always be another guy. Maybe they can put themselves out there like that because they aren't doing it so they can feel validated. Their confidence comes from within and doesn't hinge on the answer of one guy at a bar.

I've often wondered what it would be like to know there is always someone else; to know I could get any guy I wanted. In my younger days, I truly believed no one would ever want me. I was fat and disgusting and my personality wasn't awesome enough to make up for it, which obviously meant I was going to be alone forever. My younger self was so dramatic. But when I did put myself out there and was immediately rejected, it was further proof that all those thoughts were true. It was evidence to support my belief that no one would ever want me.

Not only was I giving the keys to my confidence to someone else, but I believed my body had to be at the center of my confidence. I was basing my entire sense of self-worth on how good or bad my body was based on the opinions of people I barely even knew. I was letting the number of strangers who flirted with me at a bar, the number of boys I kissed, and the number of dates I had been on to be my measuring stick for how worthy I was of love. Based on those numbers, my self-esteem and confidence were in the basement.

It has taken me years to figure it out, but I am more than just a body. I'm more than just an object to be admired and lusted after. It took me longer than I would like to admit for me to stop basing my view of myself on my jean size and how many people I'd kissed. My body is never going to be the most interesting thing about me, and I'm okay with that. I think that statement is true for most people, because there is so much more to all of us than just what we look like. I have far more to offer the world than just a body to look at. I have talents, skills, and gifts to share that have nothing to do with my body.

I will probably never know what it feels like to walk into a bar and know I could have any guy in the room, and even if I had a reason to be putting my phone number in random guys' phones, I still wouldn't be able to do it. But that doesn't bother me anymore. My confidence is no longer a product of someone else's view of me, and my body is no longer the sole factor in determining how worthy I am because I have finally realized I am more than just a body.

CONFESSION 22

I DON'T WANT YOU TO TELL ME I'M NOT FAT

I have complained about being fat. A lot. My family and friends have listened to it for years. I have literally cried on the phone to my sisters and my friends, talking about how no one was ever going to love me and I was going to die fat and alone. I've complained about being too fat to wear certain clothes or do certain things. I've complained about being fat just because I could and inevitably always get the same response: "You're not fat!" Sometimes it's said with conviction like they really mean it or, at the very least, are pretending to mean it. Sometimes it's said with a clear eye roll behind the words. But it doesn't matter how it's said because those words can't erase my entire life of evidence to the contrary.

It seems obvious that if I've spent my whole life worrying about, thinking about, and assuming other people are judging me for being fat that the solution would be to convince me I'm not fat, right? Or maybe the solution should be losing weight so I'm not fat, but that's not what this chapter is about. It might seem counterintuitive, but I don't want you to tell me I'm not fat.

Because here's the thing. Telling me I'm not fat, when I obviously am, doesn't make me feel any better. It's not a compliment for you to tell me I'm not fat and then turn around and make rude comments about celebrities or strangers on the street that are much smaller than me. It's not a compliment for you to tell me I'm not fat and then complain about the non-existent fat roll you have on your stomach or talk about how fat you "feel," like fat is a feeling instead of a way to describe bodies like mine. It doesn't feel good for you to just dismiss my feelings and my body with a statement that isn't true.

I get it, it seems weird to respond in any other way when we've been trained our whole lives that being fat is the worst thing we could possibly be. If you don't say I'm not fat, what are you going to say instead? But most of the time, I don't need you to convince me I'm not fat. I don't need you to make me feel better about being fat. I just need you to listen, to really listen and try to understand that life in a big body is different and sometimes harder than life in a smaller body. I don't need or want you to dismiss my entire life's worth of experiences with those three words.

It wasn't always this way. As little as a few years ago, maybe even a few months ago, I would've loved it if anyone told me I wasn't fat. In fact, I probably intentionally brought up the topic in hopes that the people around me would vehemently reassure me that I wasn't fat, that I was beautiful (like you can't be both at the same time), and that I looked great. I would use their words to help make me feel better about myself, to numb the pain and hatred I felt toward my own body. If everyone I knew insisted I wasn't fat, then obviously I must not be, and what a relief that was. But just like all the other times I've looked for reassurance from outside sources, my friends and family proclaiming that I'm not fat doesn't do anything to change the fact that I actually am. It doesn't do anything to actually make me feel better about myself, and it doesn't do anything to help me accept and love my fat body.

Why do you have to reassure me I'm not fat anyway? Is being fat the worst thing I could be? Why have we been trained to shy away from having hard conversations that might actually make us grow?

What if, instead of telling me I'm not fat, we talked about why the world has convinced us that being fat is a bad thing? Or why me thinking I'm fat makes me sad? What if we talked about how the world has conditioned women to base their entire sense of worth and identities on their body size? What if we talked about thin privilege and what we can do to make sure the next generation doesn't have to spend all their time trying to convince each other they aren't fat?

What I am talking about would take a massive shift in our culture. It would require us to remove all stigma and shame from being fat, to actually accept that fat bodies exist naturally and that we aren't all just ticking time bombs of chronic diseases waiting to go off. It would require us to work toward getting rid of the biases and prejudices fat people endure, which, in the grand scheme of all the injustices happening in the world right now, seems pretty low on the list of priorities.

Can you imagine a world where you'd never have to console your daughter because she came home from school crying when someone called her fat? Can you imagine what it would be like to see every single body type represented in the media, not just the skinny ones or the ones with the right kinds of curves? Can you imagine how it would feel to finally be free from the crushing weight of expectation women carry around from the time they are little girls? Can you imagine if we talked about fat and weight like we talked about height and eye color?

I've spent my whole life feeling sorry for myself because I'm fat. I've cried a lot of tears and said a lot of swear words over it. I've spent more money than I care to count trying to fix it. I've strained relationships with my constant need to be reassured I'm not fat. I've wasted precious time and energy on constantly thinking about how to not be fat anymore and how much better everything would be when I was finally skinny. All because society and the boys in my high school convinced me that being fat was the worst thing ever. I started to associate being fat with the end of the world, and that was the lens through which I viewed life for the past 20 years. It was a distorted, ugly reality in which I was never going to be worthy of anything because I was fat.

As I've worked on my own issues and my own mindset, I've come to realize that fat isn't nearly as scary as I used to think it was. I've come to terms with the fact that I will likely always be some variation of fat and that I'm never going to be traditionally skinny or wear a jean size in the single digits. I've stopped internalizing the word fat. I might have fat, I might even be fat, but fat isn't who I am. I don't say, "Hi, I'm Paige. I'm fat," when I meet new people. Being fat doesn't define my life anymore.

It has also helped to see amazing people on social media embrace being fat. I'm not talking about those who just accept it and stop being negative toward themselves but the people who truly love their bodies just the way they are. There are people with bodies like mine celebrating their big, beautiful bodies and wearing bikinis, dancing in bodysuits, and doing yoga in their underwear. They are redefining what it means to be fat, and it's a movement I hope to play a small part in one day. It is liberating for people like me who have spent their whole lives afraid of being fat.

Me accepting my fatness, however, does nothing to change a world that has villainized being and talking about being fat. I can see my friends and family get uncomfortable when I talk about being fat like it's no big deal. But instead of exchanging silent glances and then moving on, we have to have conversations about the feelings we have and the experiences we share. I can guarantee we all have more in common than we think we do. I don't know a single person who hasn't struggled with feeling or thinking they are fat. I'm no longer uncomfortable with being called fat, but until that is true for every single person on this planet, we have to keep having the hard conversations. We have to keep challenging the stigmas we've created and continue to perpetuate. We have to keep celebrating bodies of all shapes and sizes and stop using words like fat in a derogatory way.

For the most part, I've stopped complaining about being fat. My husband still hears it from time to time when I can't make the voices in my head shut up. If you happen to hear me complain about it, I no longer need you to lie to my face in order to avoid an uncomfortable conversation. I no longer need you to convince me that I'm beautiful even though I'm fat. I no longer need you to tell me I'm not fat. I am fat, and I'm okay with that now.

CONFESSION 23

BEING LOVED DOESN'T MAKE MY INSECURITIES GO AWAY

I used to think that if I had a boyfriend or someone who loved me, all my insecurities would go away, I'd be filled with confidence from their love, and I'd finally stop hating my body. I couldn't have been more wrong. I have an awesome husband who truly loves me just the way I am and tells me regularly how beautiful I am, but his love and acceptance does absolutely nothing to help me love and accept myself.

It makes sense when you base your worth on the opinions of other people to think that finding someone who loves you, puts up with all your quirks, and isn't repulsed by seeing you naked would make you feel better about yourself, and in some ways it does. But finding love is not a magic pill for curing self-hatred. It is not going to suddenly make you love yourself. In fact, not loving yourself is going to challenge that love and your relationship.

I've been with my husband for 10 years now. I felt nothing but hatred toward my body for seven of those years. Despite his constant assurances that I'm not disgusting, that he truly does find me attractive (insecure me used to ask him at least once a month), and that he loves me just the way I am, I still couldn't shake all the insecurities I had.

When we met, I was at a really low place in my life. I was still recovering from the sting of being rejected months before, and I was desperate for love and affection. His attention and desire made me feel worthy for the first time in my life. I can admit now it wasn't the healthiest way to start a relationship. I was also the lowest weight I had been since my freshman year in college. But as we got more comfortable with each other, I spent more time hanging out and eating pizza and less time working out. My weight crept up, and all those insecurities came flooding back. Was he going to leave me because I was too fat? Did he really think I was pretty, or did he just say that because he thought he had to? Surely he could do better than me, so why was he still here?

A few years into our relationship, my negative self-talk was at an all-time high. It didn't matter that I had a loyal, loving, attentive person by my side. It didn't matter that he had nothing but positive things to say about me, even when I gained 80 pounds. It didn't matter that our relationship got better and better through the years, even as my weight and body continued the roller coaster of weight loss/gain I had been on my whole life. None of it mattered; I still hated my body. I still stood in front of the mirror and wished to be a much smaller version of myself. I still imagined what it would be like if I could just cut all my fat off. I still wondered if he would love me more or if our relationship and sex life would be better if I were skinnier.

I would still stand in front of the mirror and critique everything I saw, even if he had complimented that very same feature earlier in the day. I still felt self-conscious about my fat and cellulite and did my best to hide it. I still felt uncomfortable when I was naked. I still didn't believe I was beautiful or worthy of being loved. I was still afraid every single day that I would wake up and it would all be gone, that he would eventually realize I was fat and unlovable. It makes my heart hurt to write these words because I know those feelings impacted our relationship. It makes my heart hurt because I know there are girls all over the world, praying and hoping and wishing for someone to love them so they can finally love themselves, and I know the harsh reality I had to endure is waiting for them.

As a girl growing up in a small, religious town, I had been taught that marriage and finding a spouse was one of the most important things I could do. In small-town Utah, girls often marry young, and I can't count how many times I was asked if I had a boyfriend when I'd go home to visit in my first few years of college. Once I did have a boyfriend, the questions quickly switched to when we were getting married. Everyone was shocked when we had a year and three-month long engagement. I was 24 when I got married and was one of the last girls in my graduating class and the class behind me to get married.

I'm not a hater of marriage, but I don't believe finding love and getting married should ever be the only focus or goal of a young girl. I don't believe marriage should be our only topic of conversation when we talk to them because that sends the message that the most important thing they can do is find a partner and be a lovable wife. It sends the message that getting married will solve all your problems when that is far from the truth.

But I believed that message. I believed that if I could find someone to love me, all my body woes would be gone. And when that didn't happen, I felt even more like a failure. If my husband loved me and accepted my body just the way it was, why couldn't I do the same thing? My fat rolls and imperfections didn't bother him, so why did they still bother me? I had finally received the validation and love I had been looking for all my life, so why didn't I feel better about myself? Why did I still let any perceived rejection shake me to my core and leave me crying myself to sleep?

I had to learn the hard way that no one's love can make you love yourself. Let me say that again for the people in the back. *No one's love can make you love yourself.* It doesn't matter how much someone else loves you, it doesn't matter if they praise you like the goddess you are and tell you every single day how beautiful and sexy you are, if you don't believe it yourself, none of it will matter.

The negative way I viewed myself negatively impacted my relationship in those first seven years. A husband or wife or boyfriend or lover shouldn't have to be continually questioned about their devotion and attraction because of their partner's insecurities. I'm not talking about partners who neglect and never show affection. I'm talking about the kind of husband who hands out compliments, who shows love and affection as mine does, but still gets interrogated on the regular about what they love about me, if they think I'm sexy enough, and why they think I'm pretty. No one should have to constantly defend their love.

This doesn't just go for romantic relationships, it goes for friendships and even family relationships too. My mom has loved me with her whole heart from the time I was a tiny 6-pound, 5-ounce baby, but her love wasn't able to keep me from learning to hate my body. Her love wasn't able to make me love myself. It doesn't matter how many times I've had friends tell me I look awesome; it didn't matter because I couldn't take their confidence in me and use it as my own.

Confidence and self-worth have to come from within. Sure, it might make you feel amazing when someone tells you "you look good," but that isn't true confidence. That is the kind of confidence that other people control, the kind that can be destroyed with one sideways glance from a stranger. Love works kind of the same way as feeling good in a new outfit. You can ask a million people if your new jeans look good, but it doesn't matter if every single person tells you how amazing you look because if you don't believe it yourself, you are never going to feel good in those jeans. Love is the same. It doesn't matter how many amazing people you have in your life telling you they love you, that love will do nothing to make you feel better about yourself if you can't find a way to love yourself first.

It took me a long time to realize all of this because I didn't know how to find confidence in myself and how to separate my worth from the opinions of other people.

Here's the thing I learned once I finally started to love myself: it made all my other relationships better. I no longer depend on the people I love to fill up my cup, and I no longer place my worth and happiness in their hands and hope they are in the mood to counter all my insecurities with compliments. I am finally able to enjoy their love and affection in a way I never had before because I'm not relying on them to give me the confidence I was lacking. I finally see what they had been seeing all these years, which is that I am worthy of love and affection regardless of the insecurities I feel and imperfections I see.

Being loved by someone else didn't erase the faults I saw in myself, and I still struggle with feeling insecure, but I've finally realized it's not someone else's responsibility to make me feel good about myself. That one is on me.

CONFESSION 24

IF I STOP TRYING WILL YOU THINK I'M FAT AND LAZY?

I've reached a point in my life where I have accepted my body. It has been a LONG time coming, but I am here. Sure, I would like to lose some weight and fit in all the clothes I wore before I got pregnant the second time, but it's not my sole focus anymore. I try to eat healthy most of the time because when I only eat pizza and ice cream I feel like crap. I work out when I want to, but it's not a way to punish myself anymore. I'm not on a diet. I eat ice cream and cookies and pizza and tacos. I drink wine and lattes from Starbucks that have way too many calories.

I'd like to tell you I've made peace with my decision and am giving the mental middle finger to everyone who thinks I *need* to lose weight, but that's just not true. I still wonder what my family and friends think. If it eat two pieces of pie at Thanksgiving, are they going to think I'm letting myself go? Is everyone thinking I've "given up" and am resigning myself to a lifetime of being fat?

It is really hard to overcome that feeling of needing to lose weight.

Even if I am comfortable in my body right now, a lot of times I still feel like I should be trying harder to weigh less. I still get the feeling that there are people I love and respect who think all my body positivity talk is really just a cover-up for choosing to be fat and lazy and happy about it.

I have spent so much of my life trying, mostly unsuccessfully, to lose weight and keep it off. I have gotten help and suggestions from well-meaning family and friends along the way; everything from diets that have worked for them, to workouts, to them trying to listen when I talk about the one millionth diet program I'm starting. I've literally been actively trying to lose weight since I was a 13-year-old and now, almost 20 years later, I'm over it.

I've talked about wanting to lose weight, about needing to lose weight, and about weight loss being my goal for so long. Is anyone going to believe me if I tell them I've stopped? I'm not even close to any sort of goal weight, and I haven't lost a bunch of weight recently, so it feels weird to stop trying and just let my body be. What would it feel like to not have a weight loss goal and to not have a smaller pair of jeans hanging out in my closet taunting me because they don't fit yet? What would it feel like to truly, 100 percent accept my body and stop trying to change it once and for all? What would it feel like to not be on a diet or talking about going on a diet for the first time in 20 years?

I am still firmly in the plus-size category and have a lot more fat than some people will deem healthy. I have absolutely no doubt that there are people I love and respect and spend my time with who think I need to lose weight or should be trying harder. I want so badly to tell those people to go to hell, but the reality is I still want their approval. How do you stop trying when the words to lose weight from every person, some of whom you love most, still echo through your head? How do you stop trying when you are still trying to convince yourself that your body is good just the way it is? How do you stop trying when you've been trying for almost two decades?

You hear those stories of people who throw their scales away and say it is the most freeing thing they've ever done. But the thought of doing that gives me anxiety. How am I supposed to know if I'm making progress if I'm not weighing myself at least once a week? I can't track my progress and tell everyone how much weight I've lost if I don't weigh myself. If I can't tell you how much weight I've lost, then obviously I'm not trying hard enough.

It's not just the idea of people thinking I'm fat that bothers me. I've gotten to the point where it's less about being fat and more about being lazy. I come from a super competitive, active family. We were athletes growing up, some of us still are, and it's hard to deal with the thought that they might think I've let myself go or that I might not be able to keep up and compete anymore if I don't lose 50 pounds. It's hard to think I might be the fat, lazy one of the family. It's hard to think I've probably always been the fat one in the family, and I was being delusional in thinking I could be anything else.

Does it really matter if I can still run up and down a basketball court or that I'm never going to be as skinny as my little sisters? Is it really going to be the worst thing ever if I never get to wear a jean size smaller than 16? Is it really going to be the end of the world if I never reach my goal weight? I know the answers to those questions and dozens more can't be found with all the people I'm worried about disappointing and embarrassing. I know the answers to those questions can only be found inside of me, but they're buried somewhere under the worry of failing to live up to the expectations and standards of others.

I was raised to never give up and not be a quitter. I was always taught I could do anything I put my mind to and that I could reach my goals if I just worked hard enough, but in the case of being skinny, I'm beginning to think that's just not true. I'm starting to think some goals aren't meant to be achieved, and sometimes it's okay to give up. Because what is achievable for some people might not be achievable for others. I know people who have competed in bodybuilding competitions less than a year after giving birth. I can confidently say no matter how hard I work, no matter how hard I try, I'm never going to be able to compete in a bikini fitness competition, especially not a year after having a baby.

Maybe it's not about giving up but switching the focus. Maybe it shouldn't be about losing weight and being fat. Instead, maybe it should be about being healthy. True health, not the diet industry definition of "health." Maybe it should be about exercising and moving my body because it feels good, not because I have to. Maybe it should be about doing it for me and not them. Maybe all the things I thought mattered are nothing in comparison to how I feel about myself and how I show up for my boys and my husband.

Maybe my mental health and sanity, and the mental health of girls and women everywhere, is more important than trying to lose the last 10 pounds or even the first 10 pounds. Maybe we should stop automatically grouping the words fat and lazy together and assuming one goes with the other. Maybe we should stop trying to force our ideals on other people and let them live the life that makes them the happiest, regardless of whether or not they are the size we think they should be. Maybe, just maybe, I might find a freedom and happiness I never imagined out there by giving up.

CONFESSION 25

I'M STILL LEARNING HOW TO LOVE MYSELF

If you've read the whole book up to this point, you know by now that it took me a long time to get here. To get to the point where I know my worth and know it has nothing to do with the opinions of other people or the size of jeans I'm wearing. To be comfortable in my own skin with or without your approval. To know that I am beautiful just the way I am right now. But I've also learned there is not a stopping point when it comes to self-love and acceptance. There is no point where I can say "I made it." There are going to be struggles and backslides and times when the self-hatred creeps back in. It's going to be a lifelong learning process.

Case in point, I make my husband take photos of me anytime my hair looks good and I have on a cute outfit because Instagram. At least 50 percent of the time, my very first thought when I look at those photos is, "God, I look fat." Or "My legs look giant." Or "I should've sucked my fat roll in further." More than half the time, my very first thought is tearing myself down because I'm still working on this whole body positivity thing, and that's okay. This is just the beginning of my journey.

Unfortunately, posting a picture of your fat rolls on Instagram with a few body positivity hashtags isn't going to suddenly make you love your fat rolls. It's not a switch you can just turn on and all of a sudden feel positive about your body. It doesn't mean you wake up one day and decide you are going to love yourself and everything is magical for the rest of your life. I can attest to the fact that this is not true.

It's impossible to simply forget everything I've experienced in my life related to confidence and body image and self-worth. It's impossible to ignore all the messages coming from a world that still values thin bodies over fat ones and is still firmly entrenched in diet culture. I know how hard it can be to let go of and work through a lifetime of insecurities and voices telling you you aren't good enough. Body positivity, self-love, body acceptance, and building confidence all take work. It's a lot of hard work battling the beliefs you've held about yourself for years and years. And sometimes that work sucks.

For a long time, I hated everything about myself. I look back on those years of my life and feel sad for that girl who missed out on truly experiencing all life has to offer because I was too focused on achieving some impossible ideal. I was too focused on how many calories something had instead of just being with the people I love and enjoying our time together. I was too focused on what other people thought of me in every single situation. I was too focused on my body and its size to focus on anything else.

Those kinds of thoughts and feelings don't go away overnight, and there are many days I still have to fight really hard to keep from slipping back into that place of all-consuming hatred. There is always going to be someone ready to tell you why you aren't good enough, skinny enough, or pretty enough.

Even when it comes to body positivity, there will be people who say I'm not doing it right. There are many body positivity advocates out there who make it seem like body positivity has to be all or nothing. You either love your body or you hate it—there can be no in-between—and if you don't love everything about yourself, you are failing.

That is an incredibly toxic and limited way to view something that has the potential to be beautiful and life-changing. Being able to look at my body in a more positive light has literally changed my life. I'm happier, more confident, am a better mom and wife, and I take risks and do things I wouldn't have done in the past, like writing this book.

I wholeheartedly believe in the power of body positivity and loving yourself, but those feelings are not with me 24/7. I don't always love my body; some days I have to intentionally drown out the negative voices in my head with positive thoughts. Some days it takes a lot of effort to not stand in front of the mirror and just cry, but that definitely doesn't make me a failure. This is a journey, and I firmly believe there is a wide range of emotions and feelings along the body positivity spectrum. There is room for doubt and uncertainty about your body because there is no such thing as perfection. Just like there is no perfect body, there is no perfect way to do body positivity.

In the past, I used to think confidence was something people were born with, but I've come to believe confidence, self-love, and being positive about my body are skills. They are things I can work on and improve on, and like almost any other skill, they require practice to get better, keep up, and maintain. I wish more than anything it was easier than that. I wish I could tell myself how

awesome I am and how much I love my body and that would be
the end of it, that would be the end of the struggle, but it doesn't
work that way. This is both good and bad news. It means that if
you are in the darkness of self-hatred, there is a way out. You can
learn to love yourself, even if it seems impossible. It's a skill I truly
believe anyone can learn, but it also means you have to be willing
to do the hard work and practice.

Body positivity and self-love are things I have to practice every
single day. I've stopped myself in the middle of a negative thought
thousands of times and will probably do it thousands more times in
my life. And it is really, really hard. There are many days when it
would be easier to stop fighting and just let the negativity win.

I read an Instagram post the other day that said working out and
eating healthy are easy, but dealing with all the stuff in our head is
so much harder, and I couldn't agree more. Dealing with the
emotions and feelings of inadequacy and trying to figure out
where all of those thoughts come from takes work. It requires
taking a hard look in the mirror and admitting all the ways I have
been enabling myself all these years. It means admitting how all
my hang-ups have negatively impacted me and how I've held
myself back for years and years. I can blame the media for only
showing skinny people and boys from high school for calling me
fat, but how I internalized those things and let them tear me down
is all on me. And that is hard to admit. That can open a whole new
can of negative self-talk if you let it.

But it's not just how I talk to myself. I've shared dozens of
examples in this book of how I've let the words, actions, and
thoughts I assumed people were having about me impact my life
and the way I viewed myself. I'm still learning how to let go of that
negativity as well, especially all the things I *think* people are
thinking about me. I would like to think there will be a time in my

life when we stop judging each other based on body size and stop insulting each other through social media, but I'm not particularly hopeful it will happen while I'm still alive. I could choose to continue letting those comments, whether made about me or not, influence how I view myself, but I can tell you that is not the kind of life I want to live anymore. Life is way too short to let thoughts you don't even know are real have an actual effect on your life.

I'm not perfect. I still let other people's opinions bother me. I still get upset at myself when I think I ate too much. I still stand in front of the mirror and wish I was skinnier. I still try on everything in my closet some mornings. I still say horrible things to myself sometimes. But those thoughts are becoming less frequent, those feelings aren't quite as strong, and I can actually look in the mirror and list a handful of things I really truly love. I can say I love myself and mean it. I can go out with friends or family and not worry about my outfit one single time. I can eat a donut without immediately feeling like a failure. These may seem like small things, but for me, they are a complete 180 from how I used to live my life. It feels like a huge weight has been lifted off my shoulders.

I've come too far to stop now. Learning to have confidence, self-esteem and loving myself is going to be a lifelong journey, but it's a journey I'm more than happy to go on, and I can't wait to see where it leads me.

CONCLUSION

WE HAVE TO DO BETTER

I f you are still reading, I want to say thank you. Thank you for reading and for listening to my stories. I hope with all my heart that you can take even one nugget from these pages and use it to make your life better. If I've inspired even one of you from all the nights sitting on my couch crying as I wrote this, it will have been worth it.

Writing this book helped me realize that I still have a long way to go when it comes to body positivity, self-love, and growing confidence. I've never shared with another soul many of the things I wrote about in these confessions, and for the first time ever, I am letting them out into the light of day. Writing about them has been healing for me in a way; it's taken a lot of self-reflection, and I've learned a lot about myself along the way. I've learned that I harbored a lot of negative feelings and self-hatred based on nothing more than the perceived thoughts of other people. I let thoughts and opinions I created in my own head and then projected onto everyone I knew control a lot of my life. I've held on to hurtful memories and judgments from the past and have been carrying the enormous weight of them for my whole life. I've let them weigh me down and make me feel bad about myself, and it is freeing to finally let them go. I've realized I sabotaged myself in so many ways. I can see that now. I can see how much my own self-sabotage kept me stuck in a cycle of self-hatred and sadness. Writing this book has made me see how much of my own misery was self-created, but I've also realized it's not all my fault.

This isn't a self-help book, but I'm going to end it with a call to action anyway. For far too long, we as a society have placed too much worth on body size and weight, especially when it comes to women. We have conditioned women and girls of every size to hate their bodies and believe they aren't enough through advertisements and magazines filled with only one type of body. They're bombarded with messages about how to get the perfect body, how to lose the last 10 pounds, or how to get six-pack abs. We have billion-dollar diet, beauty, and health and fitness industries that feed us lies about what is acceptable and then prey on the insecurities they created to make money.

We have people of all ages doing incredibly harmful things to their bodies in the name of beauty and being skinny. We have young people taking their own lives because of the bullying and constant comparison game that is happening on social media. We are living in a culture where no one feels like enough.

None of it is going to change until we do. Not until we start teaching our sons and daughters that there are more important things than what a woman's body looks like. Not until we start teaching them that women are more than objects to be looked at and that beauty isn't the most important thing. Not until we start teaching them to truly love and accept their own bodies and to know they are worthy of love and acceptance, no matter what size their jeans are.

Nothing is going to change until we stop judging and shaming each other both on social media and in the privacy of our own homes. Nothing is going to change until we realize there is a human being with feelings and emotions on the other side of our hateful comments. Nothing is going to change until we redefine what beauty means and move some of the focus away from our bodies. Nothing is going to change until we open up a dialogue and start talking about the toxic culture we've created. Not until we remove the stigma and shame from words like fat.

Yes, I am 100 percent responsible for my own reactions and feelings to everything from media advertisements to comments on my own Instagram page. Yes, how I let those comments impact me and my self-worth is totally on me, but a person can only take so much. A person can only be told so many times that they are ugly and worthless before they are going to believe it. A person only has to see the same "perfect" body type represented a few times before they feel the need to try everything in their power to fit that mold if they want to be accepted. A person can only withstand so much pressure before they fold.

I'm not just talking about women in their 30s like me. I'm talking about the little girls and teenagers who are growing up in the age of social media. The girls who are watching us tear each other down and learning from our example. Teenagers who have to deal with bullying and hurtful comments to their face and then go home and get it from every side of the Internet. Teenagers and children who are learning what is acceptable and what is not from the bodies we use in advertising. Teenagers and children who are suffering higher rates of mental illness and suicide than ever before.

When I was growing up, I only had to deal with the hateful things people would say to my face, but now kids get it from everywhere with no reprieve. We have to do better for them. We have to do better for the little girl who is already crying herself to sleep at night because she's too fat. We have to do it for the teenager who is starving herself so she can be skinny and pretty and loved. We have to do it so our daughters and sisters and nieces can grow up in a better world than we did so they can know they are loved and worthy no matter what.

You might be wondering how much impact you can have as one person. I can tell you from experience that it's a lot. Sometimes all it takes is to see one person loving themselves to realize it's okay for you to do the same. Sometimes all it takes is one tiny ray of hope to break through the darkness someone else is experiencing. And if enough of us band together and demand change, we can make it happen.

We can create a future where models are as diverse as the people they are selling to and where body size and shape aren't used as a measuring stick for worthiness or success. A world where we don't need a movement to love and appreciate our bodies. A world where the biggest girl in the group doesn't even realize she's different because differences are accepted and loved. A world where there are no fat friends, just friends.

ACKNOWLEDGMENTS

This book has been living inside me for over three years now. I have been taking notes on my phone about different "confessions" and ideas I've had since my now-four-year-old was a baby. It is both terrifying and exciting that it is finally out in the world. Confessions never would've become anything other than ideas on my phone if it weren't for a few people.

Mom, I know this book wasn't easy for you to read. It's taken me 30 years to realize I was never alone in my pain and struggles, you were always there silently hurting with me and praying for me even when I didn't recognize it. Your unconditional love and support has pushed me and helped me grow in ways you'll never know. I wouldn't be the person I am today without you. Thank you for always being there for me and for loving me even when I couldn't love myself.

Heather, thank you for giving me the push I needed to finally start writing this book. Your encouragement and excitement all along the way have been the catalyst I needed to share my stories with the world. I can't thank you enough for sparking that in me.

Nicole, thank you for your endless encouragement, brainstorming sessions, and believing in me even when I didn't always believe in myself. Thank you for your thoughtful feedback and unwavering support. Your friendship means more to me than I could ever adequately express with words.

John, I couldn't do any of this without you. Your continued love and support, even when it's not always convenient or easy for you, means the world to me. Thank you for being my person and helping make my crazy dreams a reality.

To all my friends and family that continue to support, encourage and love me every single day, thank you. Christina, Emily, Marissa, Mike, Morgan, Sammie, Shelby, Whitney... and many more I don't have the space to list, thank you. You'll never know how much having you in my corner means to me.

Kimberly thank you for taking my rough and sometimes jumbled thoughts and helping me turn them into something readable. Your editing and grammar skills are top-notch and I consider myself lucky to have you as both an editor and author friend.

Judi, thank you for another beautiful cover. Your work is truly incredible and I'm grateful to have someone as talented as you on my team. Thank you for always being able to bring my books to life with very little direction from me. You have an uncanny ability to take just my blurb and turn it into something amazing.

Thank you to all the badass women out there on social media inspiring others to embrace their beautiful selves. It would take too long to list them all here (you can find a portion of the list on my website), but there are truly powerful and inspiring women out there giving the world and it's "beauty" standards the middle finger and empowering others to the same. Following these people has helped me gain the confidence and bravery I needed to write this book.

And last but certainly not least, thank YOU. Thank you to every person who got excited when I talked about this book on social media, every person who said they couldn't wait to read this book. Even if you didn't know it, your excitement helped keep me going when finishing this book seemed like an impossible task. Thank you for buying and reading this book, it still blows my mind that people are willing to pay money for a book I wrote, so thank you, thank you, thank you. If you loved this book please consider writing a review and sharing it with your friends.

ABOUT THE AUTHOR

Paige Fieldsted lives in Utah with her husband, John, sons, Mason and Logan, and Willy the pug. She is an author, blogger, and body positivity advocate, who believes all women deserve to love and appreciate the body they are in right now, and that people of all shapes and sizes are worthy of love and respect.

When she's not writing you can find Paige dancing and singing in the kitchen with her boys, doing yoga, hanging out with family or reading. She is a lover of tacos, watching football, naps, ice cream, wine, pumpkin treats, any weather that doesn't require real shoes, and listening to music and singing as loud as possible.

Paige is a procrastinator, die-hard Patriots fan, obsessive list-maker, coffee addict and most of all, a work in progress.

You can find Paige on social media or at: paigefieldsted.com.

 facebook.com/paigefieldstedauthor

 instagram.com/paigemfh

 pinterest.com/paigemf

twitter.com/paigefieldsted

Made in the USA
Monee, IL
05 February 2020